The Great Canadian Trivia Book

THE GREAT CANADIAN TRIVIA BOOK

A Collection of
Compelling Curiosities
from Alouette to Zed

Mark Kearney & Randy Ray

Hounslow

The Great Canadian Trivia Book

Hounslow Press
A member of the Dundurn Group

Publisher: Anthony Hawke
Editor: Liedewy Hawke
Designer: Sebastian Vasile
Printer: Webcom

Canadian Cataloguing in Publication Data

Kearney, Mark, 1955-
    The great Canadian trivia book

ISBN 0-88882-188-3

1. Canada - Miscellanea.   I. Ray, Randy, 1952-
II. Title.

FC61. K43 1996   971'. 002   C96-930603-2
F1008. 3 . K43 1996

Publication was assisted by the **Canada Council**, the **Book Publishing Industry Development Program** of the **Department of Canadian Heritage**, and the **Ontario Arts Council**.

Care has been taken to trace the ownership of copyright material used in this book. The authors and the publisher welcome any information enabling them to rectify any references or credit in subsequent editions.

Printed and bound in Canada

Printed on recycled paper

Hounslow Press	Hounslow Press	Hounslow Press
2181 Queen Street East	73 Lime Walk	250 Sonwil Drive
Suite 301	Headington, Oxford	Buffalo, NY
Toronto, Ontario, Canada	England	U.S.A. 14225
M4E 1E5	OX3 7AD	

CONTENTS

11

To Catherine and Janis for their ideas and support, and especially for bearing with us during the many hours we spent discussing this book and several other projects.

ACKNOWLEDGEMENTS

Any book that covers such a wide range of items on Canada cannot be done without the help of many people. Although we were ultimately responsible for the researching and writing, we are grateful to the librarians, authors, and other experts who gave their time, answered our questions, or pointed us in the right direction. To everyone who contributed photographs and illustrations for the book, we appreciate your help.

We would also like to thank all of the editors who over the years provided space in their newspapers for our trivial pursuits in columns and articles, including Donna Maloney of the *Toronto Star*, Reg Vickers of the *Calgary Herald*, Ned Powers of the *Saskatoon Star Phoenix*, Rod Jerred of the *Oakville Beaver*, Joe McLaughlin of the *Red Deer Advocate*, and Dave Dauphinee of the *London Free Press*. And thanks to all the readers who sent us questions and information.

A special tip of our hats to Tony Hawke, who was supportive and encouraging of Canadian trivia as a book project, and to his wife, Liedewy, whose skilled editing pencil helped keep our prose flowing and our commas in place.

Finally, we'd like to acknowledge an inanimate object — the dock at Randy's cottage near Havelock, Ontario. It was here we tossed ideas back and forth, came up with interesting trivial items, and hammered out the concept for this book. Now that's a piece of trivia!

Mark Kearney and **Randy Ray**

PREFACE

The pie-in-the-face gag and the phrase "Beatlemania." The mini-skirt and the first radio quiz show. The creation of the Academy Awards and Winnie the Pooh.

You might do a double take if we told you all these items, diverse as they are, have Canadian roots. During our travels across Canada, digging through the shelves of various libraries, talking on the phone to a myriad of experts, and answering queries from readers who saw some of our newspaper articles on these and other subjects, we unearthed several surprises.

After six years of researching the weird and wonderful side of Canada, it is clear this country is not just a land famous for maple syrup, ice hockey and Trivial Pursuit. In fact, we are as good a source of trivia as you would ever want.

Like the time, not too long ago, when Canada had a plan to invade the United States. Or the nude sunbathing at Meech Lake. And the tale of the notorious doctor from London, Ontario, and later London, England, who some thought was Jack the Ripper.

Lurking not too far below the bland exterior Canada is so often accused of having, lies a rich world of oddities, accomplishments, and downright silliness.

Canadians dull? No way, eh!

HISTORICAL ODDITIES

Canada is still saddled with the image that its history is dull. We seem to lack the violent tinge that permeates much of the history of our neighbours to the south.

We aren't a major world power, we don't have dashing figures who have become the stuff of Hollywood legend; we simply thrive on peace, order, and good government.

Bunk.

As you will soon read, we had a plan as recently as 1920 to invade the United States. Our most legendary historical figure shouldn't have been hanged for treason on a technicality. And our country almost got called Ursalia.

Who knows, maybe our dull image got started because Great Britain once tried to trade us for the island of Guadeloupe.

Q. Is it true that a Chinese explorer "discovered" Canada long before the Vikings or other European explorers sailed here?

A. Leif Eriksson, Chris Columbus — move over. Make way for Hui-Shen. It's possible that the fifth-century Chinese explorer may have reached North America's western shores long before others who have made the claim.

When we think about "discoverers" of Canada and the rest of the New World (other than the native people who had been here for centuries), we usually picture Vikings braving the cold waters of the Atlantic a thousand years ago. Or the epic adventures of Christopher Columbus and John Cabot.

But what about explorers who sailed the Pacific Ocean? According to works by Chinese historians, it is possible that Hui-Shen, a Buddhist monk, made it here first.

These historical works describe a country called Fusang that bears a resemblance to the west coast of North America. Although some historians claim the description best fits Mexico, others believe it is closer to British Columbia.

Hui-Shen may have discovered Canada in 499. Apparently there were many monks at that time who were exploring new lands to spread the doctrines of Buddhism. The jury is still out on this one, but a Pacific route may well have been the first one used in the "discovery" of Canada.

Q. Was Canada considered an important colony to Great Britain from the start?

A. No. In fact, at one point there was a widely held view in Britain that Canada should be traded back to France in exchange for the West Indian island of Guadeloupe.

It may sound crazy now, but around 1761, many Britons believed acquiring Guadeloupe would be more advantageous than holding on to cold and barren Canada. The debate, covered in the pages of the *London Chronicle*, argued that Canada be given back to France in exchange for the West Indian island. Canada had been taken by the British just two years before at the Plains of Abraham.

The Guadeloupe advocates believed the sugar, coffee, and other products from the island were far better than the fur trade of Canada. In addition, Canada's bad weather meant ships could only travel here for five or six months of the year.

Some also argued that the British should have focused their conquests on the then French-held Louisiana rather than Canada. Nevertheless, Canada did have its supporters, who argued that Britain should hold onto whatever territories it had regardless of their possible worth. That argument seemed to work, and the rest, as they say, is history.

Q. Are there any sites in the United Kingdom dedicated to Canadian hero Sir Isaac Brock?

A. Brock, who died defending Canada at the Battle of Queenston Heights in the War of 1812, was a British career soldier for twenty-six years. He had commanded in British North America since 1802 and by 1811 was administrator of the government of Upper Canada.

But despite his heroics, Brock doesn't seem to have much of a presence in his homeland. He was born and raised in Guernsey, one of the Channel Islands. Despite those roots, there is little attention paid to him there.

In the Guernsey town of St. Peter Port, there are only two small indications that Brock was actually from there. A plaque on High Street, below a second-storey window, reads "Major-General Sir Isaac Brock, who saved Canada for the Empire, lived here." If you don't look up, you will miss it. The other tribute is a historical plaque erected there by the provincial government of Ontario.

In contrast, there is a museum in St. Peter Port devoted to Victor Hugo, the French novelist, who wasn't even from Guernsey but lived there for several years.

Q. Was the Rideau Canal in Ottawa ever used for wartime activities, as was originally intended?

A. The 202-kilometre waterway, which stretches from Kingston to Ottawa, was built in the wake of the War of 1812 as a wartime supply route to Kingston and the Great Lakes.

The military minds of the day thought the international border along the St. Lawrence River wouldn't

The Rideau Canal, Ottawa, Canada
[Ottawa Tourism & Convention Authority]

be safe if the Americans attempted another invasion, so the canal was constructed. It was designed to provide a secure water route for troops and supplies from Montreal to reach the settlements of Upper Canada and the strategic naval dockyard at Kingston.

The canal was built between 1826 and 1832 under the supervision of English Lieutenant Colonel John By but never served its intended purpose because the feared invasion didn't materialize. The waterway became a major artery for regional commerce, and continued to be for several decades, until the St. Lawrence Canal and railway systems were introduced in the 1850s. It was later a major route for luxury steamboats.

Today, the canal is used mainly by pleasure boats in summer, and in winter an eight-kilometre stretch close to downtown Ottawa becomes the world's longest skating rink.

Q. Is it true the Hudson Bay Company gives the queen a traditional payment each year of elk and beaver pelts?

A. While it is a colourful story, and one we would like to be true, the answer is no. Barry Agnew, vice-president of sales promotion at The Bay, says the company's original charter in 1670 called for it to give two elk heads and two black beaver pelts whenever royalty visited what was known as Rupert's Land. The elk and the beaver are in the company's coat of arms.

There is no record of any royalty receiving this gift until 1939, says Agnew. In fact, the gifts have been given to a visiting member of royalty on three occasions — in 1939 to King George VI, and in 1959 and 1970 to Queen Elizabeth II. On the last occasion, however, the queen was given the live animals instead, which were then donated to a zoo in Winnipeg.

The gifts were never an annual payment. The Bay has not given this gift since 1970 and does not provide gifts of any sort to any dignitaries.

Q. Did Canadians fight in the American Civil War?

A. For starters, the Civil War took place from 1861 to 1865, several years before Canada was officially formed, in 1867. Nevertheless, Fred Gaffen of the Canadian War Museum in Ottawa says that thousands of people from the territory that would become Canada, fought in the historic war waged over slavery and the economic rivalry between the industrial North and the agricultural South.

Records of "Canadian" participation in the war weren't kept, but Gaffen says historians have estimated that between 1,000 and 40,000 people, many of them immigrants from Ireland and England, were involved. He notes that most fought with the North because they opposed slavery or because they wanted to work and settle in the U.S. North. Many became American citizens after the war.

Gaffen states that some blacks from the area surrounding what is now Windsor, Ontario, joined the war, as did many French people from Lower Canada, later the province of Quebec.

Q. What names, other than Canada, were suggested before we officially became a country in 1867?

A. Although we ended up with the name Dominion of Canada, there were several others discussed at the time, in the press as well as among politicians and citizens.

Some of the favourite suggestions were New Britain, Laurentia and Brittania. A union of the Maritimes had also been discussed, and Acadia was the front-runner name for that. It was also considered a possibility for the entire country.

Other suggestions included Cabotia, Columbia, Canadia and Ursalia. By agreeing to the name Canada, both Lower and Upper Canada had to change their names, to Quebec and Ontario respectively.

Q. What is the difference between the French and English versions of "O Canada"?

A. "O Canada" was proclaimed Canada's national anthem on July 1, 1980, one hundred years after it was first sung. The music was composed by Calixa Lavallée, a well-known Quebec composer, who was asked to compose music for French lyrics written by Judge Adolphe-Basile Routhier. It was first performed on June 24, 1880, at a banquet in Quebec City.

Over the years, many different English lyrics were written to accompany Lavallée's music, but not until 1908 did a version catch on. It was written by Montreal lawyer, and later judge, Robert Stanley Weir, and after being published in an official form for the Diamond Jubilee of Confederation in 1927, it became the official English version.

A Special Joint Committee of the Senate and House of Commons recommended changing the Weir lyrics by replacing two of the "Stand on guard" phrases with "From far and wide" and "God keep our land." In 1980 Governor General Edward Schreyer proclaimed the "Act respecting the National Anthem of Canada," making "O Canada" — with the recommended changes — an official symbol of the country.

The English and French versions are of equal length, but the French version is quite different from the English, says a spokesperson with the Department of the Secretary of State of Canada in Ottawa. There have been several literal

English translations of the anthem, but one of the best is taken from *Songs of French Canada: Translated into English* by a Montreal writer William McLennan, who died in 1904.

It goes like this: "O Canada! land of our sires/Whose brow is bound with glorious bays/The sword thy valorous hand can wield/And bear the Cross that faith inspires/What mighty deeds hast thou beheld/An epogee of glorious sights/The faith, thy shield through all thy days/Shall still protect our homes and rights/Shall still protect our homes and rights".

As you can see, it differs greatly from the "stand on guard for thee" words that English-speaking Canadians sing.

The Public Information Office at Parliament Hill states that the federal government acquired the copyright for the music and English words in 1970.

Q. Was the last spike made of some precious metal to mark the completion of the CPR?

A. Rumour has it that the last spike, which was driven into the ground to mark the completion of the CPR main line in 1885, was made from solid gold. We can tell you that Canada's railroad barons of the 1880s never considered

The Hon. D.A. Smith (Lord Strathcona) driving the last C.P.R. spike on November 7, 1885.

marking the spot with a gold spike, but they did consider silver.

It was not to be, however. Lord Lansdowne, Canada's governor general at the time, had a silver spike made for the occasion. But when he went to British Columbia, he found that he had arrived several months early, when there was still a gap of twenty-eight miles in the unfinished rail line.

The last spike, when hammered home by Donald Smith of the CPR at Craigellachie, British Columbia, on November 7, 1885, was neither gold nor silver. It was iron.

Q. Is it true Louis Riel should not have been hanged for treason because he was not a Canadian citizen?

A. The argument against treason is a good one. When Louis Riel, the Metis leader, staged the rebellion in 1885, he was a citizen of the United States. Although Riel was born in the Red River settlement of what is now Manitoba, he later became an American. During his life, Riel was elected an MP, staged a number of uprisings, and also spent time in a facility for the mentally ill.

In 1878, he left Canada and travelled extensively through the United States. He joined the Republican party there and became a citizen. When he was tried for staging the rebellion, his lawyer wanted to have him plead not guilty by reason of insanity. Riel would not agree and was eventually found guilty and hanged.

Some of the charismatic leader's supporters have argued that he couldn't have been guilty of treason against Canada because he was not a Canadian citizen at the time.

Q. What was Canada's first overseas war?

A. The Boer War, fought from 1899 to 1902. According to Fred Gaffen, a senior historian at the Canadian War Museum, approximately 8,000 Canadians served during that war, with about 7,000 of them seeing action in South Africa. The rest performed garrison duty in Halifax.

Gaffen says that this was the first time a Canadian contingent was sent overseas. The soldiers served as part of the British army but as Canadian soldiers. The estimated cost to the government in fighting the war was about $3 million. During the war 89 were killed, 135 others died by accident or disease, and 252 soldiers were injured. Canadians across the country, including a number of RCMP officers, volunteered to serve in the war, he adds.

Q. Why did Canada's World War I fighter pilots wear silk scarves around their necks?

A. Despite suggestions that World War I pilots, Canadian and otherwise, wore the scarves (a) to be fashionable and (b) to wipe engine grease from their goggles, Ottawa military historian Ben Greenhous says pilots wore the flowing scarves around their necks to prevent discomfort caused by swiveling their heads to check for trailing enemy aircraft.

Greenhous explains that World War I open-cockpit aircraft didn't have rearview mirrors, and that pilots, therefore, had to turn their heads regularly from side to side in order to look out for enemy planes coming from the rear. The constant head-turning caused chafing when the pilots' coat collars rubbed on their necks, so the pilots donned the scarves to prevent irritation.

Q. Is it true that Canada once had a plan to invade the United States?

A. It sounds far-fetched these days, but as recently as in the 1920s, the director of Military Operations and Intelligence at Canadian Army Headquarters drafted a plan calling for such a tactic.

James Sutherland "Buster" Brown had joined the army in 1906. He served overseas in World War I and in the twenties took up the director's post where he drafted Defence Scheme Number 1. Under the plan, Canadian mobile columns would strike southward into the United States to capture such "key" bases as Seattle and Minneapolis. This would stall the American army from moving northward and allow time for the British army to arrive and help us.

Brown was descended from Loyalists and was described as "deeply suspicious" of Americans. Although few people, including soldiers, took the scheme seriously and Brown was later dismissed from his post, Canada had long had a fear of American invasion throughout the nineteenth century and up to World War I. And according to one historian, the Americans had a hypothetical plan for conquering Canada in the twenties as well. It was called the U.S. Army's Strategic Plan Red.

Kind of makes you think twice about free trade.

Q. Did Newfoundland have its own national anthem before joining Confederation?

A. It's more properly referred to as a colonial anthem and was titled "The Ode to Newfoundland," says Frank W. Graham, author and historian. He wrote a history of the anthem in 1979 entitled *"We Love Thee, Newfoundland,"* which is a line from the chorus of the song.

The song began as a poem in 1901 by an Englishman, Sir Cavendish Boyle, who came to Newfoundland at the turn of the century. The poem was first set to music by a German named Krippner, and that version of the anthem was performed first on January 21, 1902, at a theatre in St. John's by an actress, Frances Daisy Foster of Halifax.

According to Graham, this version didn't catch on with the public, however. A niece of Boyle's, who was a musician, suggested to him that other music should accompany his poem. On her urging, Boyle contacted an old school friend, Sir Charles Hubert Parry, a noted musical composer in England. Boyle sent the poem to Parry who obliged by sending two compositions for use as a possible anthem.

"He [Boyle] left it up to the niece to select the better of the two compositions that Parry sent," Graham states. Eventually, this version caught on with the public and it was legislated as Newfoundland's anthem. "The Ode," as it is commonly known in the province, is still sung at official functions.

Q. Was the Red Ensign ever Canada's official flag?

A. No. While the Red Ensign may have been Canada's recognized flag, it was never the country's official flag.

Consisting of the ensign of the British merchant marine, with the Canadian coat of arms added to the fly, the flag was approved for official use on government buildings in 1924. It was carried by Canadian athletes at the Olympics and by Canadian troops in World War II, before being replaced by the Maple Leaf Flag in 1965 after a lengthy and sometimes bitter national debate.

The Red Ensign, bearing the appropriate coats of arms, is now the official flag of Ontario and Manitoba.

Q. Is it true that Canada almost didn't get the chance to stage Expo 67 in Montreal?

A. Absolutely. Although Expo 67 eventually came off and was one of the most successful world's fairs ever, the right to hold the event was first given to Moscow. A Canadian senator, Mark Drouin, had visited the world's fair in

The Bandshell, Expo 67, Montreal, Quebec, October 1967.
[NAC/PA-152441]

Brussels in 1958 and came back with the idea that Canada should stage a similar event to celebrate its centennial.

Although Canada would be celebrating its one-hundredth birthday in 1967, the Soviet Union would be celebrating its fiftieth anniversary since the famous Revolution of 1917 and also applied to be the site of the fair.

A vote was held to determine the site, and Moscow won by a margin of sixteen to fourteen. Within a year of winning, however, Moscow pulled out of staging the fair because of the high costs. Canada reapplied, and on November 13, 1962, Montreal was given the rights to hold the world's fair.

Expo 67 was something of a pinnacle in Canada's modern history, and more than 50 million visitors from around the world came to visit the fair, the theme of which was Man and His World. Some of the more famous visitors included Princess Margaret, then U.S. president Lyndon B. Johnson, the Shah of Iran, and Princess Grace of Monaco.

Q. How many Canadians fought in the Vietnam War?

A. Exact figures are difficult to obtain, but the most widely accepted estimate is that some twenty thousand Canadians served with U.S. troops in the Vietnam War. Many of those fighting crossed the border voluntarily and signed up, while other Canadians were living in the United States and were drafted.

Yvon Roy of Montreal, who was wounded in the war, organized a tribute to these veterans in the late eighties. The Canadian Armed Forces does not officially recognize the voluntary involvement of Canadians who fought in Vietnam.

Q. *Who was the ill-fated Great Lakes steamer the* Edmund Fitzgerald *named after?*

A. The *Edmund Fitzgerald*, which sank during a vicious storm on Lake Superior on November 10, 1975, was named after the president of the Northwestern Mutual Life Insurance Company, which owned the ship. The family of Edmund Fitzgerald had long been involved with Great Lakes shipping, and Fitzgerald's grandfather and his five brothers skippered several vessels.

 The seventeen-year-old ship was owned by the Milwaukee-based insurance company but was under charter to the Columbia Transportation Division of the Oglebay Norton Company of Cleveland at the time of its demise. Its wreckage is located about seventeen miles northwest of Whitefish Point, in Canadian waters, slightly north of the Canada-U.S. boundary.

 In 1994, some searching expeditions were done of the ship and the twenty-nine-man crew that went down with her. The tragedy later became the subject of a hit record by Canadian singer Gordon Lightfoot.

THAT'S ENTERTAINMENT

If it weren't for Canada, the world might not have Winnie the Pooh, the Oscars, and if we stretch a bit, the old pie-in-the-face gag and quiz shows.

Canadian culture isn't something that has been restricted to our borders. Writers, actors, and musicians have made their mark around the world. For the lowdown on these and other weird and wonderful Canadian contributions to the world of entertainment, keep reading.

Q. Was the Uncle Tom of the book Uncle Tom's Cabin *from Canada?*

A. Not quite, although Reverend Josiah Henson, on whose life the character was based, moved to Upper Canada in 1830 and stayed there until his death in 1883.

Henson was a black slave born in Maryland in 1789. He escaped to Upper Canada via the Underground Railroad, and in 1841 he and other slaves, Quakers, and Abolitionists, purchased more than two hundred acres of land near what is now Dresden, Ontario. On this land they established a vocational school for fugitive slaves, a sawmill, and a grist mill. Many former slaves settled here, and today it's a popular tourist attraction.

In 1849, Henson narrated his life experiences to Harriet Beecher Stowe, who wrote the book *Uncle Tom's Cabin*. The novel, based on these experiences, was published in 1852 and eventually caused a stir worldwide. Within a year, more than three hundred thousand copies of the book had been sold.

Although many blacks returned to the United States from Canada after the emancipation of slaves in 1863, Henson remained in his new home, and when he died, he was buried nearby.

Q. I've heard that the old pie-in-the-face gag, seen in so many silent movies, was a Canadian invention. True or false?

A. Well, we can't be 100 per cent sure that some angry baker in medieval Europe didn't toss a pie at a customer and get a laugh first. But there is a written record of a Canadian coming up with the gag we are familiar with today.

Although Canadian Mack Sennett was one of several silent movie directors who popularized the pie in the face, the honour of invention goes to fellow countryman Thomas (Doc) Kelley, who had a popular travelling medicine show in the late nineteenth century.

The story goes that Kelley was in Newfoundland in 1889 when he saw a hotel stable boy being chased by an irate cook holding a piece of pie. Although the pie hit the boy's shirt and made a few onlookers laugh, Kelley gave the incident more thought. He concluded that a pie in the face would be even funnier.

As he said to a companion, "How about a whole pie, big and juicy, deliberately and carefully pushed smack into his face? How long do you think these folks would laugh then?"

Judging by the number of times the gag is still used, Kelley's pie in the face was no "pie-in-the-sky idea".

Q. Has a Canadian author ever won the Nobel Prize for Literature?

A. Yes and no, depending on how you define Canadian. Saul Bellow, an American author, was awarded the Nobel Prize for Literature in 1976.

Although an American citizen, Bellow is Canadian born. He was born in Lachine, Quebec, in 1915, and lived there until 1924 when his family moved to Chicago. Among his books is *Humboldt's Gift*. Several other Canadian writers, such as the late Robertson Davies, get mentioned each year by literary critics as possible candidates, but so far no Canadian has won.

Canadians have been awarded other Nobel Prizes, however. Among the most famous recipients are Sir Frederick Banting for medicine and Lester B. Pearson for peace.

Q. When and where was the first movie publicly shown in Canada?

A. There are two answers, says a spokesperson from the National Archives of Canada. The most widely accepted answer is that the first showing took place in Ottawa on July 21, 1896, at a place called West End Park (now Holland Avenue). A group of movies were shown by Belsaz the Magician (his real name was John Green) as part of his act during a fair held to attract potential homeowners to the area.

"The whole business of firsts is extremely difficult," the spokesperson says, however. There is some controversy as to the actual date of the Ottawa showing. Some claim that a private screening took place a day before what is recognized as the first showing. In addition, there is some evidence to suggest that there was an even earlier show in Montreal. The first public showing in the world of a film on a screen took place in Paris, France, in 1895, and the new art form spread from there.

Peter Morris in his book *Embattled Shadows*, states, however, that the Montreal claim has no factual support. Some have suggested that movies were shown in Montreal in the spring of 1896, but Morris backs the claim that the Ottawa showing was the first.

None of the films screened were more than a minute long, and they had no stories to tell. One of them was *The Kiss*, which featured May Irwin, a Canadian actress from

Whitby, Ontario. Admission to the Ottawa show was ten cents, and about twelve hundred people attended the first show.

For several years, movies were shown at fairs and on a temporary basis in some buildings. The first permanent movie theatre in Canada was the Theatorium, which was established in Toronto in 1906.

The Archives spokesperson says it is equally difficult to pinpoint when the first sound feature movie was shown in Canada, but it would have happened soon after a similar event took place in the United States. Although the talkies became popular in 1927 with the movie *The Jazz Singer*, as late as November 1928 there were only two theatres wired for sound in Toronto. Through the late twenties, movies were made in both silent and sound versions, he adds.

Q. What instrument did bandleader Guy Lombardo play?

A. Lombardo and his Royal Canadians were noted for their smooth big-band style known to legions of fans as "the sweetest music this side of heaven." The band gained fame

Guy Lombardo.

[Photo courtesy: Guy Lombardo Music Centre]

by ushering in the New Year each year to millions of North Americans who either saw them live in New York or watched on television.

Lombardo, who was born in London, Ontario, in 1902, was primarily a violin player. He and his brothers formed a small band when he was still in his teens. At that time, Lombardo was more a player than a conductor. As the band grew in size and popularity, he began conducting. In his early years he still clung to the violin and conducted with his bow. Eventually, however, he would simply use a conductor's baton. The famous bandleader, who was also a speedboat-racing champion, died in Texas in 1977.

Lombardo's violin is on display at the Guy Lombardo Museum in London, Ontario.

Q. Is Winnie the Pooh really named for Winnipeg?

A. Yes. The "bear of very little brain" was named after a real-life cub which was called Winnipeg or Winnie for short. A Captain Harry Colebourn bought the bear cub in 1914 in White River, Ontario, and took it overseas with him to England. He named it Winnipeg after his hometown.

When Colebourn had to leave for the battlefields of France, he put the bear in the London Zoo where it became a big attraction. On returning from the war, Colebourn decided to leave the bear at the zoo. Two of the visitors to the zoo were A.A. Milne and his son Christopher, who became big fans of the bear. Milne later used the bear's name in his famous books.

In 1989, people from White River sought permission from Walt Disney Productions for the right to erect a statue of the bear. Disney, which owns the rights to any reproductions of Winnie the Pooh, granted permission to the town in September of that year.

Q. Were the Warner Brothers of movie fame Canadian?

A. Almost true. In fact, only one of the brothers, Jack, was born in Canada. Their father, Ben, had first emigrated from Poland in 1890 and settled in Baltimore, Maryland. There he took up the job of a cobbler and made enough money to send for the rest of his family.

Eventually Ben changed trades and became a peddler. This job led him to Canada where the Warners settled in London, Ontario. Jack was born there in 1892. He had no birth certificate, but he later chose August 4 as his birthdate.

Ben's business didn't thrive here, and after two years the family moved back to Baltimore and later settled in Youngstown, Ohio. Two of Jack's brothers, who got into film production with him, Harry and Albert, were both born in Poland.

The Warner Brothers film company has made hundreds of films through the years including *Casablanca* and *The Jazz Singer*, which is considered to be the first important picture with sound, as well as several television shows.

Q. Did a Canadian really invent the quiz show?

A. Yes, Alex Trebek of "Jeopardy" fame is not the only one from this country to become famous for dishing out questions and answers on game shows. Canadians have contributed many things to the world, and like it or not, we can also take credit for the quiz show.

Our research turned up the fact that Roy Ward Dickson was responsible for inventing radio quiz shows. Dickson was a former teacher who had devised a game for students to test their general knowledge.

He tried to syndicate the idea to various newspapers without success. Later during the 1930s, he decided to adapt the idea for radio where prizes would be given out to the winners. He is quoted as saying, "I pictured whole families gathered about their sets, competing among themselves, yelling out answers, actually participating in what was going on many miles away."

He bought air time on a local radio station in Toronto, and on May 15, 1935, Professor Dick and his Question Box made its debut. Within two years there were more than two hundred such quiz shows in North America.

Q. Which Canadian has won the most Academy Awards?

A. The envelope, please. And the winner is ... Douglas Shearer. Although the Montreal native may not be well known to many Canadians, he won twelve Oscars throughout his forty-one-year career. The reason for his lack of fame might be chalked up to his winning awards in the Best Sound category and in other technical areas.

Shearer worked on the first major sound film, *The Jazz Singer*, in 1927 and was the first Academy Award winner (for the movie *The Big House*) in the Sound category when it was introduced in 1930. He was nominated almost annually in the Sound Recording category throughout the 1930s and 1940s and won four more times. His last win was in 1951 for *The Great Caruso*. The other Oscars were special technical awards. Some of the better-known films Shearer worked on were *San Francisco, Strike Up The Band, Mrs. Miniver,* and *Kismet*.

Another claim to fame was that his sister was Norma Shearer, who won the Best Actress award in 1930. Norma, who was married to movie mogul Irving Thalberg, received her Oscar for her role in *The Divorcee*.

Q. Who are some of the Canadian actors who have received Academy Award nominations?

A. Kate Nelligan, the London, Ontario, native who was nominated in the Best Supporting Actress category for her role in *The Prince of Tides*, is just one of many in a long line of Canadian Oscar nominees. The first Canadian-born Oscar winner in the actor or actress category was Mary Pickford in 1929, for her role in *Coquette*.

In fact, Canadian-born actresses had a bit of a stranglehold on the Oscar for a few years running as Montreal's Norma Shearer won in 1930 for *The Divorcee* while Cobourg, Ontario's Marie Dressler won in 1931 for *Min and Bill*. Both Shearer and Dressler were nominated for Oscars in subsequent years.

Toronto-born Walter Huston (Angelica's grandfather) was nominated a few times before winning the Best Supporting Actor award in 1948 for his role in *The Treasure of the Sierra Madre*. Harold Russell, another Canadian-born actor, also won in that category in 1946 for *The Best Years of Our Lives*. Some other Canadian-born Oscar nominees in either lead or supporting roles are Walter Pidgeon, Gene Lockhart, Alexander Knox, Hume Cronyn, Geneviève Bujold, Chief Dan George, Dan Aykroyd, and Graham Greene.

Q. Is it true that a Canadian invented the Academy Awards?

A. Although not Canadian born, producer Louis B. Mayer, one of the *M*'s in MGM studios, grew up in Canada and is responsible for creating the Academy Awards.

Mayer was born in Minsk, Russia, in 1885. When he was three, he and his family moved to Saint John, New Brunswick. Mayer's father was involved in the scrap-metal industry, and after quitting school at a young age, Mayer went into the business as well. When he was nineteen, however, he moved to Boston and eventually bought into some nickelodeons, the places where movies were shown in the early part of this century. Later, he began producing films. He moved to California in 1918, co-founding MGM in 1924.

In 1926, labour negotiations between the studio bosses and others in the movie business became strained. Mayer decided to solve this conundrum by setting up an industry-wide organization made up of club members who would meet annually at a banquet and work to improve technical advances in movies and polish Hollywood's image. At the time it had been tarnished by several scandals.

The Academy of Motion Picture Arts and Sciences had a few founding members, invited others in the business to join, drew up a charter, and elected actor Douglas Fairbanks Sr. as its first president. After holding its first banquet, it was decided to establish annual awards of merit recognizing "distinctive achievement" in movie making. The awards were to be based on votes by the members.

A number of categories were decided upon, some of which no longer exist, and nominations and votes were tallied. In the early days, the awards were announced before the ceremony took place, so that there wasn't any of the tension and surprise we sometimes associate with the awards today.

Mayer oversaw most of the proceedings although he was not responsible for creating the statue we now call the Oscar. The awards were given out for the first time in May 1929.

Mayer remained a major force in motion pictures until the 1950s and died in 1957. Ironically, this "Canadian" not only became an American citizen but went around claiming falsely that he was born on the 4th of July, American Independence Day. Mayer received a special Academy Award in 1950.

Q. Is there a Canadian connection to the term Beatlemania?

A. Yes, former Ottawa music journalist Sandy Gardiner. The album *Beatlemania!* was the first Beatles LP to be released in Canada, and not only is Gardiner responsible for a quotation on the album, he is also responsible for the name of the LP.

A native of Glasgow, Scotland, Gardiner was a music writer for six years in the United Kingdom. Later, he was an editor and entertainment writer for the *Ottawa Journal*, which folded in 1980.

In 1963, while at the *Journal*, Gardiner visited Britain and wrote an article that suggested that a Liverpool foursome named The Beatles was poised to take the world by storm. He called the phenomenon "Beatlemania."

His story was spotted by Capitol Records, and the company used his term as the title of the first Beatles album sold in Canada. First released in Britain as *With The Beatles*, the LP was titled *Beatlemania!* when it hit Canadian record stores.

A few lines from Gardiner's article, along with his name, are on the front cover of the album, alongside quotations from *Time* and *Newsweek* magazines.

Gardiner's contribution reads: "A new disease is sweeping through Britain ... and doctors are powerless to stop it ... it's Beatlemania! This Liverpool group play to packed houses wherever they go ..."

Before he gave up newspaper work Gardiner interviewed members of the Beatles six times. He also managed a number of Ottawa rock-and-roll bands, including The Esquires, The Townsmen, and The Staccatos, who later became The Five Man Electrical Band.

Since 1980, Gardiner has handled public affairs for British Airways, and when last heard from was the airline's American public affairs manager and based in New York City.

Sandy Gardiner.

[Photo: Paul Friend]

Q. Why did people believe that 1970s Canadian band Klaatu was The Beatles reunited?

A. Toronto band Klaatu did indeed fool everyone back in the mid-seventies into believing they were The Beatles. Back then, music fans were eager for The Beatles to reunite, and rumours flew constantly about the Fab Four getting back together.

Enter Klaatu, made up of musicians Terry Draper, John Woloschuk, and Dee Long. They recorded an album and decided to cloak themselves in secrecy, using the name Klaatu, which was a character in the movie *The Day The Earth Stood Still*. A journalist in Providence, Rhode Island, reviewed the album and concluded that Klaatu were in fact The Beatles recording under a different name.

The journalist said that the album, including the single "Sub Rosa Subway," sounded like The Beatles and pointed to other clues to indicate Klaatu were really John, Paul, George, and Ringo. For example, Ringo had released an album with a picture of the Klaatu character on the cover. And Paul had apparently finished a concert by saying, "Thanks, and see you when the earth stands still."

Draper says the band issued denials about being The Beatles, but still maintained the secret of who they were. That only fueled the Beatles' rumours even more, and Klaatu's record sales soared.

According to Draper, it was no coincidence that Klaatu's songs sounded Beatlesque — the three tried to sound like The Beatles on some songs. "Everyone wanted the Beatles to get back together again, and so they bought the rumour. We were thrilled. That was wonderful because we were all devout Beatles fans."

Once the truth came out (*Rolling Stone* magazine named Klaatu "Hype of the Year" in 1977), the band's records didn't sell as well. Klaatu continued into the early 1980s and released a CD of the first album in 1990 and others later. When last heard from, Draper and Long were still involved in music while Woloschuk was an accountant with many musician clients.

Album cover of Klaatu's "Sir Army Suit."

[Randy Ray]

Q. Who was the Canadian member of the chart-topping American rhythm-and-blues band The Young Rascals?

A. Ottawa-born Gene Cornish played with The Young Rascals in the 1960s and his fluid guitar work is featured on hit songs like "Good Lovin'," "Groovin'," "How Can I Be Sure," "A Beautiful Morning," and "People Got To Be Free."

Cornish, who later moved to and grew up mostly in Rochester, New York, played a lot around the Ottawa area in the late fifties and early sixties, before forming a band called The Unbeatables and moving to New York City to play the famed Peppermint Lounge.

He later performed with Joey Dee and the Starlighters, who recorded The Peppermint Twist, and met Felix Cavaliere and Eddie Brigati, who joined him in forming The Young Rascals. The fourth member was Dino Danelli.

The band had nine Top Twenty songs in just over two years before breaking up when internal bickering caused a rift among members.

After leaving The Rascals, Cornish played in the group Bulldog with Danelli. The pair also teamed up to produce an album and single for Canadian band April Wine. He later played with the group Fotomaker, has written and produced songs and was last heard to have formed the group G.C. Dangerous which had some success in the New York area.

In the late eighties, Cornish toured with Cavaliere and Danelli in a reformed version of The Rascals. Although he is an American citizen and was living in New York City, Cornish still had relatives in the Ottawa area and in an interview called Canadians "the nicest people in the world ... I'm proud to be from Canada. I want people there to know that there's a part of Canada in The Rascals."

Q. Do Canadian records and albums make good collectors' items?

A. In this age of compact discs, records can still be pretty lucrative for collectors. Many Canadians have gone on to achieve national and international fame in the music industry, but some of the more obscure groups are the ones whose records are the rarest and the most valuable.

André Gibeault of Quebec has compiled a list of some four thousand singles and albums in his book *Canadian Records*. The book looks at collectibles from 1955 to 1975 and lists the price you might expect to get. Remember, however, that your records must be in mint or near-mint condition to garner top dollar, and prices may vary from buyer to buyer.

The rarest and most valuable album listed in the book is *Royal American 20th Century Blues* by Toronto rock band Rockadrome. The album was released in 1969 on the Sound Canada label and is listed as being worth $450. Other albums that could reap profits for their owners are *Sussex* by Toronto band Bent Wind, which is worth $350, *Les Différents* by Quebec group Différents, worth $250, and *Plastic Cloud* by Bay Ridges, Ontario, group Plastic Cloud, which came out in 1969 and is worth $225.

There are a number of other albums that are probably worth more than $100 these days, including *Sings Like It Is* by David Clayton Thomas who went on to fame in Blood, Sweat and Tears, and *Live at the Village Corner* by the Two Tones. One of the Two Tones gained much more fame and money later under his own name — Gordon Lightfoot.

One of the pricier singles is "Not Fade Away," which was recorded on the Moon label by popular rock trio Rush in 1973, when they were starting out. It is worth $75.

Most big name bands' work hasn't really escalated in value because many of their songs aren't rare. For example, the most you might get for a song by Calgary group The Stampeders is $15 for their first single "House of Shake."

Q. What is the story behind the French-Canadian folk song "Alouette" and its translation?

A. "Alouette" is probably the best known of all Canadian folk songs and is popular throughout the world. Interestingly enough, the song is not of Canadian origin but was brought over by the French several hundred years ago.

The lyrics are fairly simple and often repeated throughout the song. An *alouette* is a skylark, and the song is a strange one in that it is about plucking (presumably feathers) off different parts of the bird's body.

Different versions exist in various parts of Canada, but the one that is most widely sung has as its opening lines "Alouette, gentille alouette, alouette, je t'y plumerai," which roughly translates as "Skylark, gentle skylark, I will pluck your feathers." Then, each verse mentions a different part of the body being plucked — *la tête* (the head), *le bec* (the beak), *le nez* (the nose) and so on.

It doesn't leave much for the bird, but it sure keeps the singers happy.

FROM SEA TO SHINING SEA

When you live in a country that stretches from sea to sea and from the Great Lakes to the Arctic, geography becomes almost as important as history.

One book can't do justice to all the interesting places in Canada, let alone one chapter. But where else are you going to find out about nude sunbathing at Meech Lake?

Q. Does Canada own the North Pole?

A. The North Pole is not owned by any country. The Pole is the earth's northernmost geographic point, located at the northern end of the earth's axis. It lies in the Arctic Ocean, more than 7,200 kilometres north of Ellesmere Island, at a point where the ocean is 4,087 metres deep and usually covered with drifting pack ice.

A spokesperson for the legal branch of the federal External Affairs Department in Ottawa said that no country has ever attempted to prove legal ownership of the area around the North Pole. "States have particularly defined rights and no state has rights at that point. No one has ever tried to lay claim to the pole," he said.

Q. What are the Northern Lights and do they produce sounds?

A. The Northern Lights, or Aurora Borealis, light up the skies of northern Canada as a result of a collision between fast-moving particles streaming out from the sun and rarefied gases in the upper atmosphere. The collision of solar electrons and air storms and molecules produces the often incredible display of light.

The auroral lights can be seen as shimmering, pulsating curtains of green and pink lights, or as an arc of faint light stretching low across the sky, or as a diffuse glow of steady light, or as darting streamers and dancing rays that continually change their form.

Green is the most commonly seen colour; and it is created by electrons striking very cold oxygen in the rarefied upper air. Pink is produced when nitrogen is hit. In the summer, violet-gray shades are often seen as electrons rush through the very warm, sunlit portion of the night sky at high altitudes.

The lights are never closer than 65 kilometres above the earth, sometimes they are 1,000 km away, but usually they are seen from a distance of 130 km.

Consequently, anyone who claims to have heard a faint swishing, rustling, or crackling sound must be mistaken. The distance separating auroras from observers makes it impossible to hear them, even if they did create sounds — which is quite unlikely.

A possible explanation is that the aurora induces electric charges at the earth's surface that result in a multitude of small discharges at the tips of foliage. The observer watching the aurora associates the sounds with changes in the aurora, although the sounds emanate from a spot near the observer.

Q. *Where is Canada's largest island, and how many islands are there in the country?*

A. Canada's largest piece of land surrounded by water is Baffin Island in the Canadian North, with an area of 507,451 square kilometres. The second largest, also in the North, is Victoria Island, with an area of 217,290 km², followed by Ellesmere Island, in northern Canada's Queen Elizabeth Islands, at 196,236 km², and Newfoundland, at 108,860.

Fourteen other Canadian Islands exceed 10,000 km², including Vancouver Island in British Columbia at 31,284 km² and Cape Breton Island, in Nova Scotia, at 10,311 km². Various sources say the total number of islands in Canada has never been established, noting there are about 30,000 islands in Ontario's Georgian Bay alone. *The Canadian Gazetteer Atlas* (1980) records the names of 1,016 islands and 129 groups of islands, or archipelagos, and states that 259 were inhabited in the mid 1970s.

The island with the largest population, according to a recent census, is Île de Montréal with almost 1.7 million people.

Q. Does Canada have a desert?

A. Although western Canadians who have endured recent droughts might suggest otherwise, Canada has no true deserts — only regions that exhibit some desertlike features.

Deserts cover about 20 per cent of the earth's surface and are regions in which evaporation greatly exceeds precipitation, resulting in a water deficiency few life forms can endure.

The Canadian Encyclopedia mentions that examples of desertlike areas in Canada include the sandy expanse south of Lake Athabasca, which lies within a forested region with a humid climate. It formed on raised, coarse-grained, glacial deltaic deposits which retain insufficient surface moisture to allow vegetation to become established.

Smaller areas in the Canadian Arctic, exposed to strong winds and lacking vegetation, exhibit a desertlike appearance. In the driest part of the Prairies, north and south of the Cypress Hills, for example, and the most southerly parts of the Fraser, Thompson, Nicola, Similkameen, Okanagan, and Kootenay river valleys, precipitation can be as low as 250 to 300 millimetres and vegetation is of the semi-arid type, like sagebrush and rabbitbrush.

Q. Where was Canada's first oil boom?

A. You probably think that the initial activity in the oil industry occurred in Oil Springs, Ontario, or Turner Valley, Alberta, where oil was discovered in 1857 and 1904, respectively. If you are talking a petroleum oil boom, you are right.

A boom involving another kind of oil, however, took place in the Labrador fisheries, hundreds of years earlier. In the sixteenth century a full-blown whale-oil industry existed on the coast of Labrador for about five generations, between the first voyages of Jacques Cartier in 1534 and those of Samuel de Champlain in 1603.

The 1970s scholar Selma Barkham found the remains of the fisheries and primitive refineries established by the Spanish Basques in Red Bay, Labrador. Nine whaling stations employed about two thousand whalers, who for six months of the year hunted about twenty thousand bowhead and right whales, refined their oil, and supplied the product to the ports of Bristol, Southampton, London and Flanders.

Q. Where is the geographical centre of Canada?

A. It can be difficult to pinpoint exactly where the centre is, because it depends on the projections in mapping one does to account for the curvature of the earth. A spokesperson at the University of Western Ontario's Map Library says, however, that calculations put the centre just south of Southampton Island in Hudson's Bay.

She states that the point is located approximately at latitude 62.9 north and longitude 87.5 west.

This centre was calculated by taking the distance between the northernmost point, Cape Columbia on Ellesmere Island, to the southernmost point, Middle Island in Lake Erie, and finding the midpoint. Then they took the distance between the westernmost point at the Yukon/Alaska border, and the easternmost point, Cape Spear, Newfoundland, and took the midpoint. Where the two lines meet and based on the projection they used in their calculations, they came up with Canada's geographical centre.

Q. Are the icebergs that flow past Newfoundland a common phenomenon there?

A. Apart from the earth's polar regions, Newfoundland is the iceberg capital of the world. The icebergs generally float by the province from May to August and weigh an average of half a million tons. Some measuring ten million tons have been recorded.

The part of the iceberg that you see sticking out of the water is roughly one-seventh the total size. Because of their

Icebergs off the coast of Newfoundland.
[Newfoundland & Labrador Tourism – Deanne Peters, photographer]

immense size and weight, icebergs can be dangerous to any boats that come near. In fact, research scientists study the movement of icebergs to determine where and how fast they will travel, so that boats can avoid their path.

The icebergs one sees in Newfoundland have most likely flowed from Greenland and taken two to three years to make the trip. Icebergs contain about 75 per cent of the earth's fresh water, and one iceberg once drifted from the Arctic to Bermuda, a distance of about four thousand kilometres.

Q. Our nation's capital is often referred to as Ottawa-Hull. Does that mean Hull is also the capital of Canada?

A. Hull, no. Hull, which is directly across the Ottawa River from Ottawa in the province of Quebec, has acquired a sizable chunk of government activity, including the federal departments of forestry, environment, public works, and government services. But it is not considered part of the capital city.

Ottawa-Hull, Canada.

Ottawa holds the distinction of being the capital as designated by Queen Victoria in January 1858, when the city became the capital of Upper and Lower Canada. In 1867, the British North America Act designated Ottawa as the "seat" of the federal government for the new country of Canada.

Both cities, however, are part of the "National Capital Region," a 4,660-square-kilometre area which encompasses all or part of twenty-seven municipalities, with a combined population in 1995 of about 1.5 million people. The capital's commission is responsibile for developing the capital's cultural and symbolic resources and making landmarks like the Parliament Buildings more accessible to Canadians and visitors, according to a commission information officer.

Q. Is Newfoundland the only place in the world that has a half-hour time zone?

A. "The world will end at 8 P.M., 8:30 in Newfoundland" is how the old joke goes, but our easternmost Canadian province is not the only place in the world that has this unusual time-zone designation. Although Newfoundland is unique in that respect in North America, Suriname, in South America, lies in the same half hour-zone.

In the same situation are some islands in the Pacific Ocean, as well as Iran, Afghanistan, and some parts of India. Nepal is even more unusual, according to the *World Almanac*, in that it has a fifteen-minute time zone. In other words, when it is 5:30 P.M. in India, it is 5:45 in Nepal.

And that's no joke.

Q. Where are the strongest currents in the world?

A. According to the *Guinness Book of World Records*, the strongest currents are the Nakwakto Rapids at Slingsby Channel in British Columbia. The flow rate may reach 16 knots or 18.4 miles per hour.

Canada also claims a number of other water-related records. The greatest tides in the world occur in the Bay of Fundy; the world's largest bay, measured by shoreline length, is Hudson Bay, and part of the world's biggest lake, Lake Superior, lies in Canada.

Q. Why is Labrador, despite being physically attached to Quebec, a part of Newfoundland?

A. The territorial status of Labrador and the rights to ownership have been a bone of contention for almost as long as non-native people have lived in Canada. The

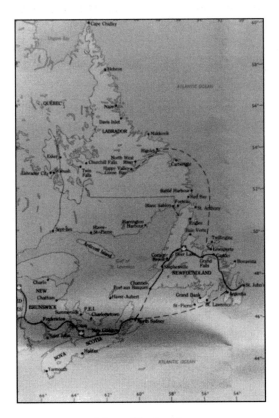

Map of Labrador.

[Photo: Catherine Blake]

boundaries of Labrador have changed several times over the year, but the region itself has been consistently a part of Newfoundland since the early 1930s.

An assistant professor in history at the University of Waterloo in Kitchener-Waterloo whose specialty is Quebec, says that the decision to designate Labrador a part of Newfoundland was made by a judicial committee of the British Privy Council. The dispute between Quebec and the then Dominion of Newfoundland was over resources, especially the development of hydro-electric power.

Before the decision, Labrador was mostly an uninhabited territory with both Quebec and Newfoundland laying claim to it. The professor says the decision favoured Newfoundland because the Privy Council committee's research of maps showed that historically Labrador had been considered part of Newfoundland.

Quebec was "extremely bitter" over the decision, the professor says, and tried to re-open the dispute again in 1949, when Newfoundland was deciding whether to join Canada. "The nationalists in Quebec were even more bitter because this part that they always thought should be part of Quebec was being lopped off."

They saw this as more evidence of how Quebec was shrinking, as it had been for more than 150 years since it was New France. "The French saw themselves as territorially always the victim of these kinds of decisions.

"There has always been this fierce hostility between the two (Quebec and Newfoundland), and it has almost always been over Labrador."

And although the car licence plates show it as Newfoundland and Labrador, the province's official name is just Newfoundland, according to the professor.

Q. If Quebec separates into a distinct country, would Canada still be the second largest country in the world?

A. Canada is approximately 9.97 million square kilometres from sea to sea, meaning we can boast that "we're number two, we're number two" when it comes to geographical size. Only Russia, at about 17.3 million square kilometres, is larger. The countries next to us in size are in descending order: China, the United States, Brazil, and Australia. Quebec is Canada's largest province and is slightly larger than 1.54 million square kilometres.

If Quebec were to eventually separate and become a different country, the size of Canada would be reduced to about 8.4 million square kilometres. That would leave us much smaller than China and the United States and just slightly smaller than Brazil.

Canada would drop from second to fifth place. We would still be bigger than Australia, which is approximately 7.7 million square kilometres.

Q. Where was the worst rainstorm in Canada?

A. According to Environment Canada, the most intense rainstorm in this country took place in Buffalo Gap, Saskatchewan, on May 30, 1961. Approximately 250 millimetres of rain fell in less than an hour. The rain and high winds washed out roads, eroded fields, and stripped bark from several trees.

By the way, the two cities that share the honour of being the thunderstorm capital of Canada are London, Ontario, and Windsor, Ontario. They average 34 thunderstorm days per year, which is light compared with Kampala, Uganda, where the average is 242 thunderstorm days per year.

Q. What can you tell me about Meech Lake — the lake, not the agreement?

A. Meech Lake, where the first version of the controversial Meech Lake Constitutional Accord was negotiated by Canada's first ministers, is located in Gatineau Park in Quebec, a twenty-minute drive across the Ottawa River from Ottawa. The lake is named after Asa Meech, a Congregationist minister from the New England states, who came to Hull, Quebec, in 1815. He eventually received title to a two-hundred-acre property at the southeast corner of what later became Meech Lake.

Asa Meech died in 1849, at age seventy-four, and is buried in the Old Chelsea Protestant burying ground near Meech Lake, where his gravestone can still be seen. His house is the oldest structure in Gatineau Park and still stands on Meech Lake Road, near the lake.

Probably the most famous building at Meech Lake is Willson House, a government-operated conference centre, where Prime Minister Mulroney and Canada's premiers negotiated the Meech Accord on April 30, 1987. The building, which sits on a hill high above the lake, is the former home of inventor Thomas Leopold "Carbide" Willson, who invented acetylene gas and later sold his patent for the gas to Union Carbide.

Willson's house is not accessible to the public but the lake can be used for boating and swimming. It also has a wooded area frequented by nudists, and its shores are dotted with a number of privately owned cottages and year-round residences.

MONEY, MONEY, MONEY

"Money makes the world go around," as one of the songs from the hit musical *Cabaret* goes.

Despite our often weak dollar, or perhaps because of it, Canadians still maintain an interest in things financial. We have researched a few pieces of monetary information you won't find in the pages of most business publications. And just because it's trivia doesn't mean it's "non-cents."

Q. Whose portrait appears on the $1,000 bill?

A. A portrait of Queen Elizabeth II is on the $1,000 Canadian bill. Her portrait also appears on three others — the old $1 and $2 bills and $20 bills. Why is the Queen so popular on our bank notes? "She is head of state of the country. We have no mandate to put her on the bills, it's just custom," says Graham Esler, chief curator for the Bank of Canada's National Currency Collection. Portraits of prime ministers are on the rest: Sir Wilfrid Laurier on the $5 bill; Sir John A. Macdonald on the $10 note; W.L. Mackenzie King and Sir Robert Borden on the $50 and $100 bills respectively. If you're wondering who decides which famous person will appear on our money, it's the federal finance minister, Esler says.

Q. How did the shinplaster get its name?

A. The 25-cent Dominion government notes were first issued in 1870, when Canada was experiencing a shortage of silver coins as a result of a tardy shipment of silver from the Royal Mint in England, according to the curator of the National Currency Museum in Ottawa. They were last issued in 1923 and remained in circulation in Canada until the late 1930s.

The curator says Shinplasters picked up their name from similar bills in the United States. "They were paid to troops in revolutionary times and had little value, so soldiers used them to wrap their leggings and keep warm." Another source maintains, however, that the nickname didn't originate until 1837, long after the American Revolution. And that it was the size, shape, and low value of the notes, which reminded people of medicinal shinplasters, that account for the name.

Shinplasters that are in average condition are worth only a few dollars today, but the curator states that some of the notes issued as part of the first series with the letter A or B on the front of the bill can be worth "hundreds of dollars" if they are in brand-new condition.

Q. How long have Canadians paid income tax and who is responsible for the system?

A. It was hardly an occasion for a party, but September 20, 1992, marked the seventy-fifth birthday of the income-tax system Canadians love to hate. Income tax came into force on September 20, 1917, as a temporary measure to help pay for Canada's effort in the First World War.

According to the history books, only the Opposition Liberals complained about the new system, but their beef was that the Income Tax War Act wasn't set high enough. The base rate was set at 4 per cent and applied to single people earning $1,500 a year and married men earning more than $3,000. There was also a "supertax" of 2 per cent on all incomes between $6,000 and $10,000, and the rate rose progressively to 25 per cent of all income above $100,000.

At the time, the average annual wage was $800, and few people were included in the $100,000 bracket, so generally speaking, the tax applied to only the wealthiest 10 per cent of the population. When the tax hit its tenth anniversary, only 119,000 Canadians, less than 2 per cent of the population, needed to file a return and the tax brought in $4.1 million, barely 16 per cent of total government revenues.

By comparison, 19.7 million Canadians filed returns in 1993, paying income taxes of $117.6 billion, levied at combined provincial/federal rates of 45 to 69 per cent of taxable income.

Q. I have half of a Canadian $20 bill. Is it worth anything?

A. Don't throw your half of the bill away — it's worth $10. A manager of operations for the Bank of Canada in Ottawa says damaged Canadian paper money — even bills that are burned in a fire — can be worth all or part of their face value, depending on how bad the damage is.

Torn bills are worth full value if three-fifths of the note remains intact. If between two-fifths and three-fifths is

A Canadian $20 bill.

[Photo: Catherine Blake]

intact, the bill is worth half its value, and if you have less than two-fifths of the bill, it is worth nothing.

Bank of Canada officials determine how much a damaged bill is worth by placing it on a piece of plastic the same size as the bill. The plastic is divided into a grid, or series of squares, which allow the bank to accurately calculate how much of the note is intact.

Bills that are burned to ashes in a fire can also be worth their full face value, he said. If a stack of bills goes up in smoke, the Bank of Canada has special scientific tests that can determine how many bills were burned and what denomination each lost bill was. The tests are often used when stores or other businesses lose money in fires.

"Your money may have gone up in smoke but don't throw away the ashes," the official advises.

Q. *When was the original $1 coin, the silver dollar, first circulated?*

A. As popular as silver dollars are with collectors and others, the Canadian government and the Royal Canadian Mint had many problems introducing them.

The 1935 Canadian silver dollar.

In his book *Striking Impressions*, James Haxby writes that two $1 pieces were struck by the Royal Mint in England in 1911 and sent to Canada as patterns for the new silver dollar. The mint in Canada was anxious to proceed but the government of the day denied permission. The on-again off-again existence of the silver dollar continued mostly because it was feared the public would not accept the coin and the mint would incur a huge loss. But in October 1934, Prime Minister R. B. Bennett decided Canada should finally issue a silver dollar the next year to mark the silver jubilee of the reign of King George V and Queen Mary.

The issue would capitalize on allegiance to the monarchy to ensure its acceptance, and it would simultaneously help the silver-mining industry and allow the government to bask in the much-needed patriotic glow during those depressed times.

The coin, nicknamed "the George," featured the crowned head of George V on one side and a picture of a voyageur and a native paddling a canoe on the reverse.

When the new $1 coin was introduced in 1987, silver dollars, by then made of nickel, were taken out of everyday circulation. The only "silver" dollars still made consist of 92.5 per cent sterling silver and 7.5 per cent copper. They are available in commemorative sets.

Q. How much Canadian money is in circulation in Canada on a given day, and where is it?

A. It is impossible to come up with a precise answer, but we did manage to discover some ball-park figures on Canada's money supply.

Spokespersons for the Bank of Canada and the Royal Canadian Mint in Ottawa estimate there is about $26.3 billion in Canadian bank notes and coins in circulation every day in Canada — $24.5 billion in paper money and $1.8 billion in coinage. That comes down to 1.1 billion bank notes and 1.2 billion coins.

But where exactly that money is can be difficult to pinpoint.

The Bank of Canada declares that paper money is in the hands of commercial businesses, in banks, in people's pockets, in safety deposit boxes and under mattresses, but could not say where the majority of bills are located. A spokesperson for the mint said 10 per cent of Canadian coins are replaced every year to keep the supply consistent. "We do it because at least that many coins are lost, buried, or hidden away in drawers," she said. "For example, the mint stamps 987,000 new 50-cent pieces every year, and many end up in coin collections."

Q. How long does Canadian paper money stay in circulation and what happens to bills that get too old to use?

A. The larger the denomination of the bill, the longer it lasts, says a currency research adviser with the Bank of Canada in Ottawa.

Five-, and ten-dollar bills are in and out of our pockets and wallets the most, so they wear out faster and are taken out of circulation after about a year. Twenty-dollar bills last 2.2 years, 50s last 2.3 years, and hundreds, seven years.

Thousand-dollar bills, which few Canadians ever lay their hands on, last 10.5 years. The Bank of Canada prints about one billion bank notes a year, and approximately the same number are destroyed every year, when they become soiled, limp, torn, or dog-eared. Bills, which are made from cotton and wood fibres, are regularly sorted by the Bank of Canada, and those unfit for continued use are shredded at Bank of Canada offices in Vancouver, Calgary, Regina, Winnipeg, Toronto, Ottawa, Montreal, Saint John, and Halifax. It costs the bank about seven cents for every new note issued.

AND NOW SPORTS FANS ...

"He shoots, he scores," may be the most popular refrain in Canadian sports history. But our accomplishments aren't limited to the hockey rink.

That is not to say some of the following questions don't deal with our national pastime — but we can't forget the glory days of cricket, women's baseball, and our Olympic gold medals in soccer and the fifty-six-pound throw. And would you believe the Hamilton Tiger-Cats beating the Buffalo Bills in a football game?

Q. Has hockey always been the most popular sport in Canada?

A. Although hockey is considered Canada's national game, its role as an organized sport only truly began in the 1870s. Once it gained a foothold, hockey grew in popularity and, today, remains the most popular spectator, sport.

Prior to that, however, there tended to be a stronger British influence on the games Canadians played, according to Alan Metcalfe's book *Canada Learns to Play*.

For a good part of the nineteenth century, cricket was a particularly popular sport in Canada. It was most widely played and watched in what was then called Upper Canada, especially in Toronto. The sport grew in the 1840s and 1850s, and by 1858 the game boasted fifty-eight clubs across what would soon become the province of Ontario. As evidence of its appeal, Metcalfe notes that there were ten clubs within forty miles of Sarnia alone.

But cricket remained essentially an urban game which relied on English immigrants to maintain its prominent role, and didn't spread widely in rural regions.

As Canadians looked more and more toward their neighbours south of the border as the century progressed, the British influence began to wane. Eventually, baseball became a widely played summer sport and, of course, lacrosse was also a well-liked pastime here.

Q. Did Canada introduce football to Americans?

A. Several short-lived expansion teams in the United States in the 1990s wasn't our first foray south of the border in the sport. Canada can boast of many things, and it is true, to some extent, that we had a hand in teaching Americans about the game that evolved into what we know as football. In the mid-1800s, soccer and rugby were played here. The two balls used for the games were slightly different, with the soccer ball being round and the rugby one being slightly oblong.

According to the book *Canadian Football* by Frank Cosentino, students from McGill University introduced the game of rugby to players from Harvard University in a game in 1874. In fact, two matches were set up between the two teams. In the first one, the Harvard round ball was used, and in the second the McGill oval ball was to be used. The oval ball was lost, however, and the round one was used again, but the playing was done under McGill's rules.

The game ended in a scoreless tie, but the Americans were impressed enough to adopt the game, and the editor of the *Harvard Magenta* called it better than "the somewhat sleepy game now played by our men." The game spread throughout both countries with different rules being used. The Americans, however, can take credit for introducing the forward pass to the game.

Q. How did ice hockey get its start in Canada?

A. Canada's national game probably originated with stick-and-ball games first played on ice in northern England, according to some sources. British soldiers brought the traditions to Canada early in the nineteenth century, and versions of the games bandy and shinty were played on ice by British troops garrisoned in Halifax and Kingston in the 1850s.

There is evidence that New York Dutch and New Englanders played a game similar to hockey during colonial times. The word "hockey" may have been derived from the French *hoquet*, shepherd's crook, referring to the shape of the stick. The nickname "shinny," for informal hockey, comes from the game's origins in shinty. The games played in Canada, New York, and New England were formless affairs, and ice hockey as we now know it was first played in Montreal in 1875, with a set of rules formalized by J.G.A. Creighton, a McGill University student.

Substitution of a flat wooden disc, or puck, gave players more control. In 1879, the first organized team, the McGill University Hockey Club, was formed and with the advent of a basic set of rules, the sport quickly spread across Canada. Early hockey was played mostly outdoors on patches of natural ice with nine players per side and no forward passing of the puck.

The first "world championship" was held in 1883 at the Montreal Ice Carnival and was won by McGill. The first national association, known as the Amateur Hockey Association of Canada, was formed in 1886, with representatives from Quebec City, Montreal and Ottawa. The first Stanley Cup game was played in March 1893 and won by Montreal AAA. The Ontario Professional League was Canada's first openly professional league. The National Hockey Association was formed in 1909 and was reorganized in 1917 as the National Hockey League.

Hockey match at McGill University, Montreal, Quebec, 1901.
[NAC/PA-C17831]

Q. Did Lord Stanley do anything of importance beside donate the hockey cup that bears his name?

A. Frederick Arthur Stanley, or Lord Stanley as he later became known, was Canada's governor general from 1888 to 1893. He has been described as a publicly shy and

Lord Stanley of Preston, Derby, 1893.

"careful" governor general. Stanley's main claim to fame of course is the Stanley Cup, but he also served as a member of Parliament in Britain from 1865 to 1886. He became a member of the House of Lords as well.

During his tenure as the Queen's representative in Canada, he was a strong advocate of closer ties between Canada and Great Britain.

He has another claim to fame, however. According to one source, Lord Stanley participated in the first known sound recording in Canada. He recorded in 1888, with the new technology, "A Message to the President of the United States of America."

Q. The 1994 lockout of National Hockey League players almost meant no Stanley Cup playoffs. Has that ever happened?

A. A players' strike or lockout has never caused a Stanley Cup series to go undecided, but in 1919 illness wiped out the Stanley Cup finals. That year, when the NHL was only two years old, the black flu epidemic swept North America, killing thousands of people and taking its toll on professional hockey.

Montreal was playing against the Seattle Metropolitans when many of the players fell sick during game five, in which the Canadiens evened the series at two wins each and a tie. The next game was to be the final match to decide the cup winner but at least five Canadiens, including superstar Newsy Lalonde, found it impossible to skate.

Seattle refused the Canadiens' request to use substitute players from Victoria and, as a result, officials had no choice but to cancel the remaining game. This is the only time a Stanley Cup Series has been undecided. Montreal player Bad Joe Hall, who took sick during game five, later died of his illness in a Seattle hospital.

Q. What was boxing champion George Chuvalo's record when he finally hung up the gloves?

A. When the Canadian champion and heavyweight contender finally stepped out of the ring for good, he had won seventy-nine fights, lost fifteen and tied two. Seventy of those wins were by knockout. Chuvalo, who holds the distinction of never having been knocked down during a career that spans more than twenty years, became Canadian heavyweight champion in 1956 and was once ranked as high as the number two contender for the world title. Perhaps his most famous fight was in 1966 against reigning champion Muhammad Ali. The fight went the distance, and Ali called Chuvalo the "toughest man I ever fought."

Q. Why is five-pin bowling so popular in Canada?

A. The five-pin game was invented in Canada by Thomas Ryan (1872-1961). Ryan had gained some fame in 1905 by setting up the first ten-pin bowling alley in Canada in Toronto. Among his patrons was Sir John Eaton. It seems that regulars at the alley complained that the sixteen-pound bowling ball for the ten-pin game was too heavy.

According to information provided by the Canadian Sports Hall of Fame, Ryan tinkered around with the game and eventually came up with the five-pin version which uses a much smaller and lighter ball. The game is unique to Canada and is one of the most popular pastimes in this country. In fact, there are approximately 525,000 league bowlers and another one million occasional bowlers in Canada.

Q. If I get hit by a puck at a National Hockey League (NHL) game, what legal recourse do I have?

A. The steps you take after the incident are generally up to you, says an NHL spokesperson. There is no standing policy as to what the league will do, and it is up to you to decide whether to take legal action.

"In almost every case, when they [fans] get hurt, they usually get a lawyer," according to the spokesperson. She stated that people who take legal action usually name a number of different people in their lawsuit, including the league, the arena, "even the security guard or the hot-dog vendor. You'd be amazed."

In most cases, the action is settled out of court. Every situation is different, and each case is dealt with differently, the spokesperson added. And even though arenas post signs or issue warnings that they assume no responsibility for any injuries sustained during a game, "that's not reality. It sounds good, but it's not reality."

The NHL has no figures on how many people get hit during the season, but "if anything, I think people are more careful today" when a puck comes flying their way.

Q. How many Canadian players were involved in the professional women's baseball leagues in the 1940s?

A. The movie *A League of Their Own* was based on fact and released in the summer of 1992. In 1942, Chicago Cub owner Philip Wrigley had the idea of the All-American Girls Professional Baseball League as a way of attracting fans to ballparks.

Because of World War II, major-league baseball and the minor leagues had lost several of its players to the services. Ottawa journalist Jane Foy, who researched women's professional baseball from that era, says fifty-three Canadian women played in the league from the inaugural 1943 season to the last season in 1954, accounting for about 10 per cent of the women who played.

Among the Canadian standouts was Gladys Davis of Toronto, who was the league's first batting champion. She hit .322 for the Rockford Peaches. Olive Bend Little from Moose Jaw held a league strikeout record that was never equaled, according to Foy. Although the game started out with underhand pitching, it eventually evolved to overhand pitching and delighted fans with its high calibre of play.

Almost one million fans watched league games in 1948. The league remained something of a novelty in the early fifties, but lack of finances and the resurgence of the major leagues led to the women's game's demise.

Q. What were the original teams in the World Hockey Association?

A. The World Hockey Association (WHA) was officially established in 1971. California lawyer Gary Davidson was the prime mover behind the new league, which wanted to challenge the NHL for hockey fans' attention. In late 1971, WHA officials announced franchises for ten cities — Calgary, Chicago, Dayton, Edmonton, Los Angeles, Miami, New York, St. Paul, San Francisco, and Winnipeg.

Any new league, however, has its ups and downs (mostly downs), and teams of four of the cities, Calgary, San Francisco, Miami, and Dayton, were moved or sold before any games were played. Remember the Miami Screaming Eagles? Well, they became the Philadelphia Blazers before the WHA got underway in 1972. Dayton's franchise went to Houston, Calgary's went to Cleveland, and San Francisco's went to Quebec City.

By the time the first season started, the WHA had signed more than seventy NHL players, the most famous being Bobby Hull. In that first season the teams were the New England Whalers (then playing in Boston), Cleveland Crusaders, Philadelphia Blazers, Ottawa Nationals, Quebec Nordiques, New York Raiders, Winnipeg Jets, Houston Aeros, Los Angeles Sharks, Alberta (they changed the name to Edmonton later) Oilers, Minnesota Fighting Saints, and Chicago Cougars. Alberta's Ron Anderson scored the first WHA regular season goal.

There were many team changes over the years as franchises came and went. Other teams that skated in the WHA included the Toronto Toros, Cincinnati Stingers, Calgary Cowboys, and the Baltimore Blades. The first WHA champion was New England, and winning teams over the years received the Avco World Trophy.

The WHA lasted seven years; then four of the teams — New England (now Hartford), Winnipeg, Quebec, and Edmonton joined the NHL. And for WHA trivia buffs — the all-time leading scorer in WHA history was Marc Tardif, who notched 316 goals in six seasons, playing mostly with Quebec.

Q. Has Canada ever had any international success in soccer?

A. Although Canada has managed to qualify for the World Cup in the past, we are not known for our prowess in the sport. Back in 1904, however, at the Olympics in St. Louis, Canada came away with the gold medal in soccer or associated football as it was known. A team from Galt, Ontario (now a part of the city of Cambridge), the Galt Football Club, was Canada's representative and defeated an American team, the St. Rose team of St. Louis, 4-0 to win the gold.

The Galt team was led by its star player, Tom Taylor, who played right forward. The team had previously defeated the Christian Brothers College team 7-0 and thus made it to the gold-medal match.

There were other Canadian teams that had aspirations of going to the Olympics — the Berlin Rangers and a club from the University of Toronto. There were some questions, however, about the amateur status of certain members of the Berlin team. Galt defeated the U. of T. team 2-0 to become Canada's representative.

Not to take anything away from the Galt club, which is in the Canadian Sports Hall of Fame, it should be noted that the 1904 Olympics had little European representation.

Q. Who won Canada's first Olympic gold medal?

A. There are really two answers to this. The first Canadian to win a gold medal was George Orton, who was born in Strathroy, Ontario, and was the premier track runner in the world in the 1890s. When he won his gold medal in the 2,500-metre steeplechase at the first modern Olympics in 1896, however, he was competing for the American team. Canada did not send an Olympic team that year. Orton also placed third in the 400-metre hurdles. The first athlete to win a gold while competing as a Canadian was Etienne Desmarteau. He won the 56-pound throw (no longer an event) at the 1904 games in St. Louis.

Q. How did Canada fare at the Summer Olympics that were held two years apart instead of the usual four?

A. The modern Olympics began in 1896 in Athens, Greece, and were to be held every four years. After the 1904 games in St. Louis, however, some Greeks lobbied for having the Games in 1906 rather than waiting for 1908. They wanted to celebrate the tenth anniversary of the restoration of the Olympics and pump much needed revenue into the Olympic stadium built in Athens for the 1896 Games.

The International Olympic Committee sympathized but decided the Olympics should still be held every four years. It agreed, however, to sponsor an international meet in Athens in 1906. Many came to regard these as full-fledged Olympic Games, and Canada was represented there for the first time as a team. Prior to that, Canadian athletes competed individually.

Although, today, the 1906 Games are not considered to have been regular Olympics, Canadians had some success there. Marathoner Bill Sherring, the premier runner of his day, captured the gold medal in that event. And Donald Linden won a silver in the 1500-metre walk.

Linden had lost to an American who ran for part of the race. Officials agreed that the American had cheated and offered to re-stage the race. Linden showed up, the American didn't, and for some unknown reason the original race results stood.

Q. Who was the first National League Hockey player to wear a helmet?

A. Actually, this is a tough question to "hit on the head" as even the historical consultant at the Hockey Hall of Fame asserts there is no definite proof. He told us, however, that his research shows that a player by the name of George Owen was probably the first to don the headgear.

Although helmets are a common feature in today's game, it was only about ten years ago that they started to become commonplace in the NHL.

He says that Owen, however, who was from Hamilton, Ontario, was wearing a helmet when he played university hockey at Harvard in the 1920s. Owen joined the Boston Bruins in 1928 and brought his leather football-type helmet with him. The equipment didn't catch on with anyone else until the famous incident in 1934 when Ace Bailey got knocked to the ice by Eddie Shore.

In retaliation, some other players knocked Shore out. Apparently, Owen was influential in getting Shore to try a helmet for the next games. Soon afterward the entire Boston team showed up wearing helmets for a game against Ottawa, according to the consultant. The Hockey Hall of Fame knows little else about Owen's career.

Q. How did the University of Ottawa's teams get the name Gee-Gees?

A. Although people around Ottawa may affectionately refer to the governor general as "the Gee-Gee," that is not the source of the team's name. The co-ordinator of media and community relations for the university admits that the name has been a bit of a mystery to many people. Actually, the name was chosen in the nineteenth century to describe the school's colours — garnet and grey. Thus, the Gee-Gees represent the first letters of the school's colours.

Although it doesn't sound like one of the most imaginative names in sport, the co-ordinator reports that in 1888 an anonymous student wrote in a student publication: "There is nothing flashy about our colours, garnet and grey,

Gee-Gee logo.
[Courtesy: University of Ottawa (Sports Services)]

115

but in our eyes they are as venerable as the flag that braved a 100 years the battle and the breeze."

In addition, the dictionary defines the word gee-gee as a child's slang term for a horse. This may explain the varsity teams' logo, which shows the head of a horse with the letter *G* printed twice on the neck.

Q. How long have companies been producing hockey cards in Canada?

A. Although the phenomenon of collecting cards has only really taken off in recent years, cards have been produced since 1910. In the 1910-1913 period, cards were distributed in cigarette packages, and in the first year the players' photos were in colour.

Card production was suspended because of World War I. Since then, cards were distributed in cigarette packages for only one more season, that of 1924-25. During the 1920s, new candy and gum manufacturers were established who produced cards that could be exchanged by customers for other gifts. This is why cards from the twenties are so difficult to find. Cards became a regular feature in the thirties, but production was again stopped during World War II.

Hockey cards appeared again in 1951-52, and other companies such as York Peanut Butter and Shirriff Desserts got into the business. By the late 1960s, however, Topps in the United States and O-Pee-Chee in Canada were the only companies producing the cards.

In addition, you can also make a great deal of money if you have a complete set of cards from a particular season. Rated at the top are the complete set from 1951-52 (about $4,000) and from 1964-65, referred to by one expert as "the most beautiful sports cards every produced," (worth about $3,300).

Q. Did any Canadian Football League teams, before the league's expansion, ever play games against their counterparts in the United States and win?

A. The CFL has more than held its own over the years in games against U.S. counterparts. The first such game on record took place on September 28, 1935, when a team from Winnipeg (before it had the Blue Bomber nickname) travelled south of the border to play the Minnesota All-Stars. Winnipeg won 21 to 13 and a few days later beat the North Dakota Freshmen 26 to 7.

Fritz Hanson, a CFL star from the thirties who played in the games, reported that they were played using both American and Canadian rules. A number of exhibition games were played between CFL and NFL teams in the fifties, but the match Larry Robertson, a CFL statistician, has on record is the one in which the New York Giants defeated the Ottawa Rough Riders 27 to 6 in 1950.

The most recent game was a 38 to 21 victory for the Hamilton Tiger-Cats over the Buffalo Bills of the old American Football League. The 1961 pre-season game was played in Hamilton under Canadian rules. After that game, the AFL refused to allow their teams to play any more matches in Canada without league approval.

One CFL regular season game was played in Philadelphia on September 14, 1958, because of a dispute between the Ti-Cats and the Hamilton stadium officials. Hamilton beat the Ottawa Rough Riders 24 to 18 before some fifteen thousand fans. This was the only time prior to the nineties that a regular season game was played outside of Canada.

Q. Was the first game of basketball, invented by Canadian James Naismith, similar to what we see today?

A. Dr. James Naismith, the inventor of basketball, was born in Almonte, Ontario, near Ottawa in 1861. It was in the fall of 1891, at the YMCA in Springfield, Massachusetts, that Naismith devised the game of basketball to increase enthusiasm for physical education among students.

Because he had eighteen students in his gym class, the first game had nine players a side. Although this sounds high compared to the five players a side we see today, Naismith thought the game could be played by as many as forty players on each team on the court. He decided the game's objective would be to throw a soccer ball into empty boxes set ten feet off the ground. There were no boxes to be found, however, and peach baskets were used instead.

According to *Tales From Basketball's Past* by Eric Nadel, the first game was played in a gym that was only fifty feet by thirty-five feet, and it consisted of fifteen-minute halves with a five-minute intermission. Since the bottoms of the baskets were not cut out, a person had to retrieve the ball each time a point was scored (counting two points for a basket didn't happen until 1896). In the first game, however, only one point was scored, by a student named William R. Chase. Open-bottomed nets soon replaced the peach baskets.

Some of the similarities with today's game include not being able to run with the ball and not being allowed to strike an opponent. If a player committed two fouls, he would have to sit out until the next basket was scored. There were no free throws in the game until three years after its invention. Such things as dribbling, jump shots, three-point baskets, and slam dunks came later.

There is another Canadian connection to the original game. Five of the eighteen players in that first game were from Canada and helped spread the sport here when they returned for Christmas vacations in 1891.

Q. What can you tell me about the professional basketball team in Toronto before the Raptors?

A. The Toronto Huskies were one of eleven teams in the Basketball Association of America (BAA) which was formed in 1946. The BAA was the forerunner of today's NBA, which has become, in recent years, one of the most successful pro sports leagues on the continent.

The BAA and the Huskies weren't so fortunate, however. Other teams in the BAA, that first year, were the Boston Celtics, the Chicago Stags, the Cleveland Rebels, the Detroit Falcons, the New York Knickerbockers, the Philadelphia Warriors, the Pittsburgh Ironmen, the Providence Steamrollers, the St. Louis Bombers, and the Washington Capitols. Although the BAA had money and several big-time promoters as well as arena owners behind it, the league still had to compete with other pro groups at the time, namely, the American and National leagues.

The Huskies played their home games at Maple Leaf Gardens and went through four coaches and several different players in that first year, finishing in a tie for fifth in their division with the Celtics with a record of 22 and 38. Lew Hayman, former coach of the Toronto Argonauts football team, even coached one game that season and lost.

The Huskies' first coach was Ed Sadowski, who also played, but after twelve games he was traded to Cleveland, where he ended the first season as the second-highest-scoring player in the league. The BAA's leading scorer that first year was Joe Fulks, who set a then-record game high of forty-one points in a match against Toronto.

After the first year, four teams, Cleveland, Detroit, Pittsburgh and Toronto, folded for financial reasons. The various leagues continued to compete with each other until they were amalgamated into one league, the NBA, in 1949-50.

NBA basketball returned to Toronto in the 1970s, when the Buffalo Braves franchise played some of their home games during the regular season at the Gardens, and should be here to stay, now that the Raptors have been established.

Q. What constitutes a shot on goal in a hockey game?

A. Although this sounds like an easy question, there can be a number of situations in which it may be difficult to determine what is "statistically" a shot on goal.

"Anything a goaltender stops and prevents from going into the net," is the basic rule for shots on goal, states an associate director of information and statistician for the National Hockey League. "[Therefore], if the shot hits the post, it's not a shot on goal."

But what if Wayne Gretzky flips a shot from centre ice and the goalie stops it — can it be considered a shot on goal?

Yes. But the decision is up to the person in charge of keeping track of shots on goal. There are two statisticians approved by the NHL up in the press box at each hockey game keeping track of shots on goal by the teams as well as plus/minus records for each player. They decide whether the shot was dangerous enough to be considered a shot on goal, the spokesperson adds.

"There are so many hypothetical situations. But it is basically the statistician who decides what constitutes a shot on net. Obviously, if the guy shoots it from his own end and the goaltender happens to stop the puck, it's a judgment call." An indirect shot that is rifled off the boards and goes toward the net would not be considered a shot on goal.

A tip or redirection from someone in front of the net would be considered a shot on goal, however, as long as it went off a player from the side opposing the goalie in question. In addition, a goal is considered a shot on goal, and the person who touched it last (and who is on the opposing team) gets credit for the shot.

THE POLITICAL ARENA

Most Canadians turn to their daily newspaper or nightly TV news to get their political fix. We don't always like what we see (in fact, you might argue that with politics we hardly ever like what we see), but politician bashing is almost like a second national sport.

It is no surprise that there are lots of trivia associated with politics. For example, there was the night a House of Commons debate turned into a free-for-all that included singing, throwing a waste basket, and sending toy balloons into the air ...

Q. How outrageous have our MPs been during debates?

A. You can throw the image of a staid House of Commons right out a Parliament Hill window. We didn't have to search too far to find an example of outrageous behaviour by our MPs.

During an all-night debate in the House of Commons in the spring of 1878, a procedural wrangle developed and MPs not only hammered on their desks, they blew tin trumpets, imitated the crowing of cocks, threw sand-crackers, sent toy balloons into the air in the Commons, and hurled books across the room. Others sang "God Save The Queen," "Auld Lang Syne," and the "Marseillaise" (the anthem of France). The twenty-seven-hour debate also saw one MP throw a waste basket and another play a tune on a toy bagpipe as paper missiles veered across the room.

Keep those images in mind next time you watch a shouting match going on during Question Period.

Q. What is the story behind the original The Fathers of Confederation *painting?*

A. The painting, which features Sir John A. Macdonald standing amid assembled delegates at the Quebec Conference in October 1864, was done by Robert Harris. It was at this conference that the outline for the union of British North America was hammered out.

Harris, a native of Wales, was commissioned to paint the historic group portrait in 1883, almost nineteen years

Photograph of a painting by Robert Harris entitled "Conference at Quebec in 1864, to settle the basis of a union in the British North American Provinces."

[NAC/PA-C2149]

after the conference. He was living in Montreal at the time. Originally, Harris had been hired to paint a scene representing the Charlottetown Conference, which had taken place in September 1864, but the government decided the Quebec Conference should be shown instead.

He painted the final work in the winter of 1883-84 for a fee of four thousand dollars and it was first shown publicly in 1884, before being installed in the Parliament Buildings in Ottawa. The original painting was destroyed in the fire that razed the Centre Block of the Parliament Buildings in 1916, and when the government approached Harris to paint the portrait again, he refused because he was in poor health. He died in 1919.

Q. Who would run the country if the prime minister died or became ill and couldn't handle the responsibilities?

A. In the event of an incident incapacitating the prime minister, all of the duties would be handled by the deputy prime minister, says a deputy press secretary in the prime minister's office.

The deputy PM would have the power to run all of the country's affairs and would be able to make decisions in a number of key areas including finance and foreign affairs. He or she could even be called upon to decide whether Canada would participate in a war.

The deputy would also stand in for the prime minister at official functions and during Question Period in the House of Commons.

According to a researcher at the Library of Parliament in Ottawa, it has happened only once that a Canadian prime minister died in office and a replacement was appointed. On December 12, 1894, Prime Minister Sir John Thompson, the country's fifth prime minister, died suddenly and was replaced by Sir Mackenzie Bowell. Bowell, a former Conservative cabinet minister, was a member of the Senate when Thompson died. He was prime minister until April 27, 1896.

Q. Is it true that a Canadian was once prime minister of Britain?

A. Yes, the honour goes to Andrew Bonar Law, a native of New Brunswick who went to Britain and became an MP in 1900. He then succeeded Arthur Balfour as leader of the Conservatives. Eventually, Law held a series of important cabinet posts, such as chancellor of the Exchequer, and became prime minister in 1922. He was the only Canadian, and the only "colonial," to hold the post. He served only 209 days as the country's leader, however, before resigning because of bad health. He died in 1923.

Q. Who, besides members of Parliament, can mail letters free of charge, and who picks up the cost?

A. Mailing letters without stamps is a perk available to MPs, senators, the governor general and his/her secretary, the House of Commons Speaker (who is an MP), the Speaker of the Senate (who is a senator), the head clerks of the House of Commons and Senate, and the chief and associate librarians at the Parliamentary Library in Ottawa.

A Canada Post spokesperson explains that the perk falls under the Canada Post Act and covers letter-mail only. Parcels, priority post, or other post-office services must be paid for. The "letter-mail" privilege, however, covers any letters sent by MPs, senators and the others, whether it involves Christmas cards and utility bills, or a personal note to a constituent. It also allows MPs to send four "householders" a year to people who live in their ridings.

The Act also permits constituents to send mail free of charge to any MP, including the prime minister.

The spokesperson said that federal figures don't break down the cost of the free mailing privileges but stressed that the revenue lost to Canada Post is paid back by the federal government, which is — surprise, surprise — you and me, the taxpayer.

Q. Where did Parliament conduct its business after fire destroyed part of the Parliament Buildings in 1916?

A. After the infamous blaze levelled the Centre Block on February 3, 1916, the daily workings of the House of Commons and the Senate were moved to the Victoria Museum, now the Canadian Museum of Nature, which is located a short distance south of Parliament Hill.

MPs sat daily in an auditorium, while senators worked — we kid you not — out of the former hall of invertebrate fossils, explains the museum's chief of

The Parliament Buildings after the fire of 1916.
[Photo courtesy: House of Commons, Ottawa, Canada]

communications. All of the politicians' offices were also moved to the museum, which was shut down temporarily as a museum until 1920, when MPs and senators moved back into the rebuilt centre block.

Q. Who was responsible for introducing Canada's first medicare legislation?

A. Although Tommy Douglas usually gets most of the credit, the first government-prepaid medical plan in Canada — and North America — was introduced in the rural municipality of McKillop, about seventy kilometres north of Regina, on June 1, 1939, by Matthew Anderson.

According to a privately published biography, Anderson, the long-time reeve of McKillop, became convinced in the late 1920s that a health-insurance plan similar to those of his native Norway was desirable. He began to quietly lobby for legislation to establish such a plan, and after watching the suffering caused by the Great Depression in the 1930s, he became even more convinced that such legislation was needed.

The biography, written by Harold A. Longman, observes that, in 1938, the outlines of Anderson's plan were submitted to the voters of the municipality in a plebiscite and received overwhelming approval. The Saskatchewan Legislature then introduced a bill officially known as An Act Respecting Medical and Hospital Services for Munici-palities, which was often referred to as the Matt Anderson bill.

The bill allowed municipalities to collect taxes for health services, a procedure which was previously forbidden. It was passed by the legislature in March 1939 and went into effect a few months later. McKillop was the first to take advantage of this bill, thanks to Anderson's strong belief and lobbying.

Longman's book mentions that the initial annual cost per year was five dollars, with a maximum of fifty dollars per family, for which a patient received complete medical attention, including specialist services, surgery, hospital accommodation for up to twenty-one days and prescription drugs.

When the bill was passed, the *Regina Leader-Post* praised Anderson in an editorial which said that "Matthew S. Anderson's name will go down in municipal history in Saskatchewan as one who had the courage and initiative to be the first to put a new idea into practice."

Douglas introduced the concept of medicare on a province-wide basis in 1946, some seven years after Anderson's municipal initiatives.

Q. Can members of Parliament take their House of Commons chairs with them when they leave politics?

A. They can, and several have. A spokesperson for the Commons Speaker affirms that MPs who are defeated or who retire can buy the chairs they sit on in the Commons for

House of Commons chairs.
[Photo courtesy: House of Commons, Ottawa, Canada]

$900, which is exactly what it costs the government to replace them.

The chairs, on which MPs sit at their desks in the Commons, are made of solid oak and have green leather or crushed velvet on the backs, seats, and arms. MPs have been permitted to purchase them since the conclusion of the 1988 federal election.

"They are souvenirs, mementos of a member's stay in Parliament," the spokesperson says. "MPs spend a lot of time in them. They are a little piece of history."

Since the 1993 election, 110 MPs have bought their chairs. Among those who have doled out $900 for their chairs over the years are former NDP leader Ed Broadbent; former International Trade Minister Pat Carney of British Columbia; and former Environment Minister Tom MacMillan, an MP from Prince Edward Island. Carney and Broadbent retired, and MacMillan was defeated in the 1988 election.

Q. What is the origin of Rideau Hall in Ottawa?

A. Rideau Hall, Ottawa residence of Canada's governor general, was built in 1838 on a site just east of Parliament Hill, near the current home of the prime minister. The original structure was built by industrialist Thomas MacKay as a home for his family and at the time consisted of a rectangular, two-storey stone villa with a semi-circular front facing the garden.

In 1865, after the city was renamed Ottawa from Bytown and designated as the new capital of the province of Canada, the house was leased to the government as a residence for Lord Monck, then governor general of British North America and later Canada's first governor general. That year, a long two-storey wing was added.

In 1868, the house and grounds were purchased by the government of Canada for $82,000. In the time of Canada's third governor general, Lord Dufferin (1872–1878), the Ballroom and the Tent Room were built as wings on either side of the front entrance. The Minto Wing was added in 1899 to supply more living space.

In 1913, during the tenure of the Duke of Connaught (1911–1916), work was completed on the interior entrance hall and the present front entrance with its massive motif of the Royal Arms. Since then, a number of other changes have been made, most recently to the Tent Room in 1988.

Rideau Hall, which still houses the governor general, is a popular Ottawa tourist attraction that offers walking tours between April 1 and October 31, occasional garden parties, and levees that are also open to the public. Changing the Guard ceremonies take place at the site daily from late June to the end of August.

Rideau Hall, Ottawa, Canada.
[Photo: Sgt. R. Kolly – courtesy: Government House]

THE FAMOUS AND THE INFAMOUS

You don't hear too many people talking about how exciting Canadians are. Friendly, yes, caring, decent, even funny. But too often we get accused of being bland.

Still, Canada has had its share of interesting personalities. We have dug up the dirt on some of them, from criminals to a songwriter. We have even thrown a fictional character and a large elephant into the mix.

Q. Was Jack the Ripper a Canadian?

A. While he deservedly doesn't rank with great Canadians of the past, Dr. Thomas Neill Cream has been considered one of the suspects in the notorious nineteenth-century case. Cream was born in Glasgow, Scotland, but graduated in medicine from McGill University in the 1870s. He lived in London, Ontario, for a time and was suspected of murdering a chambermaid.

Cream moved to Chicago to practise medicine there and committed several crimes. He was convicted of murdering a man using strychnine and spent time in prison; he was released in 1891. Cream then moved to London, England, and gained a reputation for preying on prostitutes and poisoning several of them.

Cream was arrested in June of 1892 and later charged with murder. He was tried in October 1892, and according to the book *The New Murderers' Who's Who*, the evidence against him was overwhelming. Several bottles of strychnine had been found at his house. A jury took only twelve minutes to find Cream guilty. Cream never admitted to the murders and was hanged on November 15, 1892. Legend has it that just before he died he said "I am Jack the — ." Many have speculated that he was about to say "I am Jack the Ripper," but there is no proof.

Q. Who was the Canadian who did the first advertised radio broadcast?

A. Reginald Fessenden, who has been largely ignored by history books, was indeed the first to transmit human voices by radio. The transmission took place on December 24, 1906, from Brant Rock, Massachusetts, to some ships at sea owned by the United Fruit Company. During the program, Fessenden played a recording of Handel's "Largo," which was the first time a recording was played on radio, and he also sang and wished his listeners a Merry Christmas.

Fessenden was an inventor and innovator who rivaled Marconi in his development of radio. Although Marconi was the first to be credited with sending a wireless signal, when he transmitted the Morse Code letter *S* on December 13, 1901, Fessenden's broadcast was the first one to use voices, which is more like radio as we know it.

Fessenden was born in 1866 and later worked for inventor Thomas Alva Edison. In 1900, Fessenden claimed to have sent a message by electromagnetic waves, a full year before Marconi's transmission. Despite some setbacks, Fessenden was able to make strides in radio before making his historic broadcast on Christmas Eve, 1906.

Although Fessenden appeared to be destined for great success, he received little recognition and suffered from the conduct of partners who sold his patents to American companies without his consent. Fessenden died in 1932 in Bermuda. Unfortunately, some American books refer to this Canadian as "the American Marconi."

Q. Did poet Robert W. Service once act in Hollywood?

A. Service is best remembered for his poems about the Yukon Gold Rush days, particularly "The Shooting of Dan McGrew" and "The Cremation of Sam McGee". But he also played a small part in a Hollywood movie. Back in 1942, Service had, appropriately enough, the minor role of "the Poet" in the movie *The Spoilers*.

Robert Service in a canoe somewhere between Fort Smith and Fort Norman, 1911.

The movie, which is set in the Yukon, starred Marlene Dietrich as a saloon gal, John Wayne as a prospector, and Randolph Scott. The movie had been made three times before and was done again in 1955.

One prominent critic describes the version Service was in, saying it has "a good cast, but thuds out as average Western."

Q. I am told the prisoner who spent the longest time on Alcatraz was Canadian. True?

A. Yes, Alvin "Old Creepy" Karpis has the dubious honour of having spent the most time in prison on Alcatraz Island. Karpis, who was born Albin Karpowicz in Montreal in 1908, spent a record twenty-six years in the island prison situated in San Francisco Bay. The average prison stay there was about eight to ten years.

Although born in Canada, Karpis grew up in Topeka, Kansas, where his family moved when he was young. Despite living most of his life in the United States, Karpis remained a Canadian citizen. For that reason, he was deported to Canada upon his release from jail in 1969.

Karpis was one of a number of gangsters who captured the public's imagination during the Depression. Karpis had first been arrested for burglary in 1926, but gained fame in the early thirties as a bank robber and kidnapper, often as henchman of the notorious Barker gang. To avoid detection for his crimes, Karpis had his fingerprints surgically removed. He was involved in the kidnappings of William Hamm Jr., president of the Hamm Brewing Company, and Edward Bremer, president of the Commercial State Bank in St. Paul, Minnesota. Both kidnappings ended with the criminals getting their ransom money and returning the men unharmed.

By the mid-1930s, Karpis had become Public Enemy Number One; he was eventually arrested in New Orleans by the FBI in 1936. Although legend has it that J. Edgar Hoover personally arrested Karpis, the gangster mentions in his autobiography that several other officers were involved.

After spending time in Leavenworth prison, Karpis was sent to Alcatraz, where he was in the company of such notorious criminals as Al Capone, Robert Stroud (the Birdman of Alcatraz), and Baby Face Nelson. He left Alcatraz in 1962, shortly before the prison was shut down, and spent the rest of his time in a prison in Washington State. Karpis died in Spain in 1979.

Q. Who was the first person to drive across Canada in a car?

A. Thanks to the Trans-Canada Highway, anyone with time and patience can now make the drive across the country. But more than eighty years ago, two men set out to do what no one else had done — drive across Canada. Although the honour generally goes to Thomas Wilby, an aristocratic Briton, who made the journey to promote a coast-to-coast highway, it should be noted that he was accompanied by his chauffeur, F.V. Haney, who did most of the driving.

The two made the trip in a car made by the Reo Motor Car Company of Canada, starting in Halifax (we must remember that Newfoundland wasn't part of Canada at this point) on August 27, 1912. The two ran into car and highway troubles when they reached northern Ontario. The car was, in fact, shipped by train from North Bay to Sudbury and from Sault Ste. Marie to Winnipeg because there were no roads. At one point they enlisted the help of a farm woman who provided lumber so they could drive across a stream. The drive across the Prairies was a bit easier but, occasionally, when there were no settlements, there were no roads. When they drove through the Rockies, they sometimes had to move along rail lines. Fifty-two days after leaving Halifax and some forty-two hundred miles later, the car was guided to the edge of the ocean near Victoria and a flask of water gathered in Halifax was dumped into the Pacific.

Q. What is the story behind the poem written in response to Canadian John McCrae's famous work "In Flanders Fields"?

A. McCrae gained immortality with his famous World War I poem, and many of us have been moved by it each Remembrance Day. Edna Jaques, who wrote several volumes of poetry in the early twentieth century, was moved enough by the poem to write an answer to McCrae's words.

She wrote the poem in 1918, and it was read at the unveiling of the Tomb of the Unknown Soldier at Arlington National Cemetery in Washington, D.C. The poem, entitled "In Flanders Now," goes as follows:

> We have kept faith, ye Flanders' dead / Sleep well beneath those poppies red / That mark your place. / The torch your dying hands did throw / We've held it high before the foe / And answered bitter blow for blow / In Flanders' fields.
>
> And where your heroes' blood was spilled / The guns are now forever stilled / And silent grown. / There is no moaning of the slain / There is no cry of tortured pain / And blood will never flow again / In Flanders' fields.
>
> Forever holy in our sight / Shall be those crosses gleaming white / That guard your sleep. / Rest you in peace, the task is done / The fight you left us we have won / And Peace on Earth has just begun / In Flanders now.

Q. Why did John Wilkes Booth spend some time in Canada shortly before assassinating U.S. president Abraham Lincoln?

A. In fact, a great many Confederate spies and sympathizers spent time in Canada during the American Civil War. According to the book *Conspiracy in Canada*, Booth came to Montreal on October 18, 1864, and spent most of the rest of the month here meeting with fellow Confederates.

The Confederate Secret Service headquarters in Canada were in the St. Lawrence Hall Hotel in downtown Montreal, and it was here that men plotted to involve Canada in the war against the Northern states. At one point, about twenty-five men made a raid from Montreal into Vermont as a way of disrupting the North.

When Booth checked into the hotel, he told people he was here to do some oil speculation, but as an actor he also planned some performances and dramatic readings. He was mostly here, however, to discuss a wild plan to kidnap Lincoln and take him to Richmond, Virginia. Booth left Montreal at the end of the month but returned there in December.

About four months later, in April, Booth assassinated Lincoln and was the subject of an intense manhunt. He was killed during the hunt, and a Bill of Exchange from the Ontario Bank in Montreal was found on his body. Booth had opened an account at the bank during his October visit, and according to the book, the money deposited there was never claimed by Booth's heirs.

Another interesting footnote to history: Jefferson Davis, the president of the Confederate States in the Civil War, moved to Montreal in 1867, lived on Mountain Street, and wrote a book there.

John Wilkes Booth.

[NAC/PA-C49537]

Q. Is it true the Sweet Marie chocolate bar has Canadian origins?

A. Sweet Marie was a Canadian who lived in London, Ontario, according to London historian John Lutman in his book *The North and The East*.

American-born author Cy Warman was living in this southwestern Ontario city when, one day in 1893, he walked his girlfriend Marie home. He later strolled to a downtown park and wrote a love poem entitled Sweet Marie.

A few years later, tunesmith Raymon Moore wrote music to accompany the lyrics, and the result was a musical hit that made Marie the best-known London resident in North America.

Later, a chocolate company capitalized on the song's name and made the Sweet Marie bar. Still later, Warman proposed to his sweet Marie, she accepted, and the couple raised their four children in London.

Q. Who was "Farini, Champion of Niagara"?

A. The gentleman in question was known as G.A. Farini and first made a big name for himself in an August 11, 1864, report in the *New York Times* about his bizarre attempt to walk along the brink of Niagara Falls using a pair of stilts. A misstep almost cost the daredevil his life, but he went on to fame with a string of even zanier stunts.

Before we decribe some of his exploits, however, we should tell you that Farini was not his real name and he was not a Canadian, although he did have close ties with Canada. He was William Leonard Hunt and was born in Lockport, New York, on June 10, 1838, of Canadian parents who met in Port Hope, Ontario. After his birth in Lockport, his parents moved backed to southern Ontario, and the future stuntman was educated near Bowmanville.

Hunt's greatest joy as a boy was watching travelling circuses in the backwoods villages. He would memorize performances and practise them on homemade equipment he built in his father's barn. Eventually, he joined the Durham County Agricultural Fair, during which he walked across the Ganaraska River on a tightrope in a location in the middle of Port Hope.

Farini's career took him through high-wire performances in southern Ontario, Minnesota, and the United States Midwest before he decided to challenge another famous stuntman, known as the Great Blondin, to a high-wire walk above Niagara Falls. Later, he walked a tightrope across the falls while inside a sack and on separate occasions with a man and a washing machine on his back. He worked in South America and New York City before again tackling Niagara Falls on stilts — the trick that almost killed him. He also worked in England and with P.T. Barnum's Greatest Show on Earth.

Eventually Farini became a partner in a show-business agency and moved to Toronto with his wife. He later came back to Port Hope, where he died in January 1929 at age ninety-one. The *New York Times*, which helped boost his high-wire career, was among the newspapers to print his obituary.

Q. Does Canada have a patron saint?

A. Since many of the early European settlers were from France and also Catholic, it makes sense that Canada would have a patron saint. According to one source, Canada has two of them.

Joseph, who was the spouse of the Virgin Mary, is listed as the patron saint of Canada. He is also the patron of China, Belgium, and carpenters. Anne, who was the mother of the Virgin Mary, is listed as a patron saint of Canada as well. She is also the patron of cabinet-makers, housewives, and women in labour.

Q. Did Jumbo, the famous circus elephant who was killed in Canada, die when charging a train to protect two companions?

A. Pack that theory away in a trunk forever. The story of Jumbo charging a locomotive to save the lives of two friends is a bit of circus hokum spread by Jumbo's owner, P.T. Barnum. According to information from officials at the Jumbo Monument in St. Thomas, Ontario, Jumbo was not quite that heroic.

On September 15, 1885, Jumbo, a star attraction of P.T. Barnum's circus, and Tom Thumb, a smaller elephant, were being led along tracks in St. Thomas to their circus railway car. An unscheduled train appeared out of the fog, and the two elephants, trapped between it and the circus car, began racing along the tracks. They were overtaken by the train, and the collision derailed the locomotive and two cars.

Jumbo was thrown forward, and a tusk was driven into the elephant's brain. Tom Thumb was hurled down a bank and broke a leg. Jumbo's keeper, Scott, was by the elephant's side as it lay dying. Shortly afterward, P.T. Barnum, known for his promotional skills, began spreading the heroic story.

Jumbo was an African elephant, the first of its kind to be taken to England. Jumbo was a popular fixture of the London Zoo for seventeen years before Barnum arrived on the scene.

Apparently, Jumbo was reluctant to leave the zoo and lay down in the street refusing to budge. Eventually, the elephant was put on a ship and taken to America where it was greeted by thousands on arrival at the New York docks. A couple of months later, Jumbo began touring North America in the circus.

After the elephant's death, the hide was mounted and became a circus attraction. Two years later the hide was donated to Tufts University Museum in Boston, but it was destroyed in a museum fire in 1975. The skeleton of the giant elephant is on display at the New York Museum of Natural History.

A life-size statue of Jumbo was erected in St. Thomas in 1985 to commemorate the one-hundreth anniversary of the elephant's death.

Monument to Jumbo the elephant, St. Thomas, Ontario.
[Photo: Barry Schneider – courtesy: St. Thomas Economic Development Corporation]

Q. Who is the guy pictured on the Canadian Tire money?

A. You don't have to be the Queen or a prime minister to get your face on money. The Scottish-looking gentleman with the scarf around his neck is "Sandy McTire," and he first made his appearance in 1958, when Canadian Tire introduced its now-famous coupons. A communications assistant with the company explains that McTire wasn't based on anyone in particular but was the creation of company artist Bernie Friedman.

The idea for the coupons originated with Canadian Tire co-founder A.J. Billes, who was looking for a gimmick to entice people to use the company's newly-launched gas bars. According to the spokesperson, Billes was quoted as saying, "We chose a Scotsman because the Scottish are known for their savings and frugality, and that's what our coupons are all about."

The coupons are printed on the same material as real money, and for every dollar you spend you receive anywhere from 3 to 5 per cent back in coupons. At first, Canadian Tire money was available only from the gas bars, observes the spokesperson, but it was introduced in the company's stores in 1961.

Q. Whatever happened to Isabel Le Bourdais, the woman who created a nationwide sensation in the 1960s with her book on the Steven Truscott murder case?

A. Le Bourdais, who was named Canadian Press Woman of the Year in 1966, gained international fame with her book *The Trial of Steven Truscott*. The book outlined the facts of the 1959 murder of Lynne Harper in Clinton, Ontario, the arrest, trial and conviction of the fourteen-year-old Truscott.

Le Bourdais believed, like many, that Truscott was innocent and the trial unfair. She researched the case and wrote the book that captured the attention of millions of Canadians and people in the United States, Britain, and Switzerland.

Although an inquiry into the case was eventually launched, Truscott did not receive a new trial. He was released from prison in the late sixties, and given a new identity; he settled in Ontario where he married. He has been heard from occasionally over the years, still stating his innocence.

But what about Le Bourdais? Although she never wrote anything quite as popular, she received letters from around the world, remained in demand for interviews, and still heard occasionally from people who read the book.

"Years and years after the book, if I went anywhere and gave my name out, people would say 'Oh, you're the one,'" she said in an interview from her Toronto home. "I was amazed at how long my name stuck in their minds."

Le Bourdais worked in public relations for the Registered Nurses Association until the early 1980s and did other kinds of writing. She had a bad fall in early 1990 and broke her hip. Le Bourdais, in her eighties when interviewed, had no immediate plans to write again, but said she had a novel and six short stories that "needed work" before being published.

She said she was unhappy that Truscott was not acquitted, but that she was proud of the attention the book generated for the case.

"It was amazing, the extent that people got worked up at the time. But the most astonishing thing was that nobody wrote me a nasty letter [about the book]."

She hadn't been in contact with Truscott for some time, but occasionally talked to his mother. And as for any theories about who killed Lynne Harper, Le Bourdais said she thought it was someone who testified at the trial, but wasn't saying who. "It wouldn't do any good" unless the person confessed, she said.

"But up to this point, nobody, not any judge, not any lawyer, not any individual has been able to show how Steven could be guilty and fit the evidence."

THE WONDERFUL WORLD OF SCIENCE

Over the years, Canada has given the world insulin, the telephone, and the snowmobile.

Scientists have made many of their greatest discoveries by asking "why" or "how come?" We have taken our cue from them and added the phrase "I wonder ..." in order to unearth a few trivial oddities from Canada's world of science and technology.

Q. I have often wondered — just how do astronauts go to the bathroom when they are in space?

A. Fortunately for today's astronauts, life in space is more efficient than it used to be and there is more room to move around. Clothing is similar to what you might wear on an airplane. According to the National Aeronautics and Space Administration (NASA), the space shuttles, in which Canadian astronauts Marc Garneau and Roberta Bondar among others travelled, contain a commode and urinal. They are as Earth-like as possible and have an airflow that draws waste into storage compartments. The air is filtered to remove dirt and bacteria and vented to the vacuum of space to prevent odour formation. When the shuttle returns to Earth, the storage compartment is emptied.

The same procedure is followed for teeth brushing. After rinsing, the water is put into a waste container and stored for dumping when the astronauts land.

Q. Is there a difference between a U.S. billion and a Canadian billion?

A. Not according to a variety of mathematical sources. There is a traditional difference, however, between what a billion means to North Americans and what it means to people from Great Britain. Several sources explain that what we mean by a billion here in North America is a one followed by nine zeros or a thousand million. In Great Britain, though, and also apparently in Germany, a billion has historically meant a one followed by twelve zeros or a million million. It's what we call a trillion.

In the book *The World of Mathematics*, the authors write that the word *million* didn't seem to be in use until the thirteenth century. Although most sources state that the word *billion* is of French origin and was introduced into the English language in the seventeenth century approximately, the book's authors say that it derives from Italian and was originally written as *bimillion*. In other words, a billion was a million squared or one million million, as the British have used it.

It seems, however, that the French changed the meaning to one thousand million, and this was adopted by Americans. *The Oxford Dictionary* defines *billion* as both a thousand million and a million million. *The Gage Canadian Dictionary* states that Canadians follow the American usage.

In addition, several sources state that the American usage began gaining popularity in Great Britain in the 1950s and 1960s. And, in fact, according to one source, the British Treasury changed to the American sense of the word by the mid-sixties.

A math professor at the University of Western Ontario comments that he is familiar with the difference between the British way and the American way. He adds that mathematicians often avoid the confusion by not using the word *billion*. They refer to numbers as either ten to the sixth power or ten to the twelfth power, without labelling them *billion* or *trillion*.

Q. How much blood is in the human body, and how much would a person have to lose to die?

A. The average adult has four to six litres of blood, declares the Canadian Red Cross in Ottawa, and the bigger a person is, the more blood he or she has. A newborn, eight-pound baby, for example, has about 300 millilitres of blood in its system, which is less than the amount of beer in a full beer bottle.

The Red Cross states that the standard blood-bank donation of a unit of blood (about 450 millilitres) causes no trouble for most healthy people. Many blood banks, though, won't accept donations from people who weigh less than 45.5 kilograms, because one unit represents a greater percentage of their total supply than it does for people who weigh more.

The loss of as little as one or two units of blood could endanger the life of a particularly frail or elderly person, says the Red Cross, but most healthy people could lose about 40 per cent of their blood before they would die of blood loss — depending on how quickly they lose the blood.

The loss of 20 per cent of blood supply — more than 1,000 millilitres, or two to three units — would make a person a likely candidate for a transfusion.

Q. Is there any truth to the idea that keeping the crust piece of a sliced loaf of bread in the package as long as possible keeps it all fresh?

A. Not really, according to a spokesperson for a food research laboratory in Toronto. The overall crust of a loaf of bread has less moisture in it that the middle of the loaf. Once bread is sliced, however, and put in a plastic bag, any moisture lost from the surfaces of the slices will be kept within the package.

A loaf of bread.

[Photo: Catherine Blake]

If you open up the bag and take out the end piece first, instead of passing it by and taking the next slice, there is going to be little change in the moisture content within the package.

"[Leaving the end piece] is probably not a bad thing to do," the spokesperson said. "But I don't think it's going to make a huge difference."

The slice next to the end crust in the package may be protected somewhat more if you leave the end crust in there, but the difference is probably negligible. There really haven't been any specific tests on that, the spokesperson added.

Q. How common is heart disease in Canada?

A. Statistics provided by the University of Ottawa Heart Institute show that cardiovascular disease is the number one cause of death among Canadian adults, taking about seventy-five thousand lives annually. The institute, which is headed by world-renowned surgeon Dr. Wilbert Keon, states that about three million Canadians suffer from some form of heart disease, but most don't know it until a heart attack strikes.

Cardiovascular disease includes all diseases of the heart and blood vessels. Heart attack and stroke, the two most common ailments, are usually caused by the narrowing or obstruction of blood vessels supplying the heart and brain. This narrowing is caused by a buildup of plaque in arteries, the result of elevated levels of blood cholesterol.

The cost of health care, lost productivity, and disability related to the disease totals about twenty billion dollars a year in Canada. According to the institute, increased education about exercising, diet, and the perils of smoking have reduced the heart-related mortality rate for people under sixty-five by about 30 per cent.

Q. Who was the first person to successfully receive insulin once Dr. Frederick Banting finished experimenting on dogs?

A. Banting and his assistant, Charles Best, first successfully tried their new formula, insulin, on a fourteen-year-old boy named Leonard Thompson. The experiment took place in Toronto in January 1922, but prior to that the two had experienced several failures. It was expected that Thompson would die from diabetes, but the insulin worked in this case. Thompson ended up taking insulin for the rest of his life.

Sir Frederick G. Banting and Dr. Charles H. Best.
[Banting Museum & Education Centre]

Banting and Best had begun their experiments on dogs the previous year and were able to produce insulin from an extract of beef pancreas. Once their successes were made public, several diabetics came to Toronto to receive help. In 1923, Banting and Dr. J.J.R. Macleod, who oversaw the experiments, won the Nobel Prize. Banting shared his winnings with Best, while Macleod shared his with Dr. James Collip, a biochemist who developed a technique to purify insulin.

Q. What are some of the offbeat gadgets for which Canadian inventors can take credit?

A. If you are among those who think Canada's only significant inventions are ice hockey, Trivial Pursuit, and marquis wheat, guess again — Canadians can take credit for a wide variety of gadgetry which touches on everything from home decorating and tools to fashion and sports.

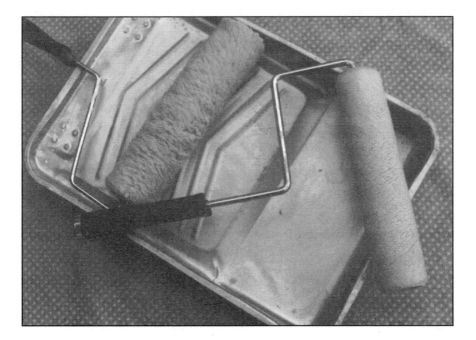

Paint roller.

[Photo: Catherine Blake]

Some of the items that might not have been around today, were it not for the innovations of Canadian inventors, are the paint roller, the mini-skirt, the Geiger counter, Pablum, engineered yarn, automatic mail-handling equipment, flight simulators for pilot training, beer cases with tuck-in handles, the zipper, the snowmobile, kerosene, and acetylene gas.

A completed snowmobile at the Bombardier Company factory, November 1953.

Q. Did Canada ever have an outbreak of leprosy?

A. A number of Canadians have suffered from leprosy, a chronic disease that causes skin to break out in sores and can leave victims disfigured, deformed, and blind. The illness has been called the disease of Biblical times and a disease of the sinner, the unclean, and the Godless.

According to newspaper stories, ignorance and paranoia concerning the afflication dictated that Canada's lepers be kept in complete isolation even after evidence showed that leprosy was not the highly contagious plague it was portrayed to be. The federal government and the Canadian public demanded leprosy victims be shut away and forgotten.

In 1849 more than fifty men, women, and children were shipped to Tracadie, New Brunswick, to an isolation hospital on the Tracadie River. Most were new immigrants to Canada and most are buried at Tracadie where their graves are marked with iron crosses. The institution was operated for much of the time by the Sisters of St. Joseph; it was closed in 1965.

In British Columbia, the tiny settlement of Bentinck Island was established in 1924 as a more humane alternative to the harsh existence on D'Arcy Island, near Vancouver Island. Of twenty-one patients, thirteen died on the island, the last, an elderly Chinese man, in 1958. The island is now an explosives-training range, but the graves have been left as a sanctuary.

Q. What causes lightning, and how often does it strike ground, buildings, or people in Canada?

A. Environment Canada's *Canadian Weather Trivia Calendar* defines lightning as the discharge of static electricity which has gradually built up within a towering cloud until it is great enough to overcome the resistance of the air and jump between charged parts of a cloud, or between the cloud and the ground.

At any given moment there are about a hundred lightning strikes over the earth's surface, totalling 32 million a year, of which at least a hundred thousand hit Canada.

Although people are occasionally struck by lightning, Environment Canada remarks that such occurrences are rare. Nine out of ten lightning discharges travel from cloud to cloud and never reach the earth, and most ground strikes cause little harm.

Nevertheless, environmental officials say that lightning, while dazzling, can also be deadly. Every year it takes about five hundred lives, causes thirteen hundred injuries and about $20-million worth of property damage in Canada and the United States. It starts about 20 per cent of all forest fires in Canada and about two thousand fires annually on private property.

Q. Did Alexander Graham Bell invent the telephone in Canada or in the United States?

A. This question rings with controversy: if you are an American you were probably taught the phone was invented in the United States, and if you are Canadian, you believe it was done here.

The answer really depends on how you define the word *invention*. Bell moved to Brantford, Ontario, in 1870 and began experiments on how to send the human voice over a wire. He moved to Boston in 1871 to teach, but kept working on his project.

Alexander Graham Bell opening the New York-Chicago long-distance line, October 18, 1898.

[NAC/PA-CK1483]

For the next three years, Bell returned to Brantford often and discussed the idea of the telephone at length with his father one night in 1874. A year later he wrote the specifications for the telephone during another visit to Brantford, but it was on March 10, 1876, in Boston that he uttered the first words over a wire: "Mr. Watson, come here, I want you."

Later that year, Bell also placed the first one-way long-distance call. This took place in Canada, between Brantford and Paris, Ontario — about eight miles away. If that doesn't settle your argument, remember that Bell often declared that Brantford was the home of his famous invention. For example, in a speech in 1909 in Ottawa, he said: "Of this you may be sure, the telephone was *invented* in Canada. It was *made* in the United States."

Q. Why is there a national historic site for Marconi in Glace Bay, Nova Scotia, if the first transatlantic message travelled between England and Signal Hill, Newfoundland?

A. It is true that the first transatlantic message was sent from England to Newfoundland in 1901 and that Guglielmo Marconi, a young Italian physicist, was involved in it. That first message, however, was a simple Morse Code signal — S.

Once that was achieved, Marconi built a transmitting station in Table Head, in Glace Bay. It was here on December 15, 1902, that he sent out a sequence of radio waves and transmitted the first wireless message from North America across the ocean to England.

The reason for the national site being there is probably that Marconi did most of his important work in Nova Scotia, and that it was the site of the first message sent from North America rather than being just a receiving point.

A few years later, Marconi enlarged and moved his radio station to nearby Port Morien, and by 1908 he was providing regular commercial overseas wireless service. The station also monitored distress signals at sea, including the one from the ship *Titanic* when it sank in 1912.

Q. Who are the volunteer weather watchers who monitor Canada's skies for the federal weather office?

A. Environment Canada relies on a national network of more than twenty-five hundred citizen weather observers to record temperature and precipitation data that describe much of Canada's climate.

Every day of the year, the team of volunteer weather spies takes observations which are sent once a month to Environment Canada's Atmospheric Environment Service for incorporation into summaries of the country's past weather, explains a climatologist for Environment Canada.

Armed with thermometers and rain gauges or rulers (depending on the season), they record temperatures and precipitation at 8: 00 A.M. and 5: 00 P.M. The climatologist adds that almost every community in Canada has one volunteer weather observer, and larger cities like Calgary, Saskatoon, Winnipeg, and Toronto have many more.

Weather watchers — who range from students, farmers and retirees, to optometrists, dentists and mayors — set up their mini-weather stations in back yards, farm yards, school yards, and church yards.

Their data is recorded in Environment Canada computers, alongside three billion weather observations gathered over the years and is used for a variety of purposes. It may be retrieved as evidence in a court case to determine weather conditions on the day of an accident, or to help farmers determine growing conditions before they plant seeds. Engineers can use the data to determine snow conditions in a community before designing a new building.

Many government and industrial organizations, power companies, agricultural research stations, and schools have added weather observing to their employees' duties, but most observers take on weather observing because of a personal interest in the weather and as a public service to their community.

Some stations have been maintained by the same families for many years, passing the task from one generation to the next. One Ontario family monitored the weather for one hundred and three years in the Muskoka region north of Toronto.

Canada's weather-watch network began more than two hundred years ago, long before a national meteorological service was set up. Missionaries, traders, Hudson's Bay Company employees, and explorers were among Canada's early volunteer observers. The earliest Canadian weather observations were taken by a Quebec City doctor between 1742 and 1756. Canada now has more than twenty-seven hundred observation stations, including some manned by federal employees.

In addition, Environment Canada has a team of about five thousand volunteers who watch for hazardous or potentially hazardous weather. These "severe-weather watchers" gaze at the clouds in search of hail, tornadoes, damaging winds, or extensive precipitation and relay sightings to a designated weather office by telephone.

Their reports give forecasters an instant reading of the severity of storms. No instruments are required, says the climatologist, "just a keen eye" for violent situations such as hail and tornadoes.

He notes that a severe-weather watcher in Leduc, Alberta, was first to sight the tornado that destroyed part of Edmonton in July 1987. The early sighting allowed Environment Canada to alert area residents twenty-five minutes before the storm swept through the area.

Q. Who was the first person to report a UFO in North America?

A. The person believed responsible for the first report of a UFO sighting was Simeon Perkins, a Nova Scotia shipbuilder and diarist.

In an entry in his diary on October 12, 1786, Perkins wrote: "A strange story comes from the Bay of Fundy that ships have been seen in the air ... they were said to be seen in New Minas ... by a girl about sunrise. The girl cried out and two men who were in the house came out and saw them. There were fifteen ships and a man forward with his hand stretched out. They made to the eastward. They were so near, people saw their sides and ports. The story did not obtain universal credit but some people believed it."

SOME FINAL TANTALIZING TIDBITS

Not everything trivial can be pigeonholed into one particular category.

Some of the compelling curiosities and tantalizing tidbits from the Great White North simply aren't easy to define. In this chapter, you will find trifles on some of our world-beating exploits, the stories behind such everyday things as your area code, postal code, and favourite drinks. Why we say "zed" instead of "zee" and the message Canada sent to the moon.

Q. Why is it that when I fly into Toronto they put a tag on my luggage with the letters YYZ?

A. The three letters don't really seem to have any connection with Toronto; to a certain extent they were arbitrarily assigned. A spokesperson for the International Civil Aviation Organization (ICAO) says that a number of codes were assigned to airports throughout the world to avoid duplication.

Canada has codes that begin with *Y, U, Z* and *W,* but *Y* is what is used for commercial airports. The other two letters define the location of the airport more specifically. The codes were mostly assigned in the 1950s, and attempts were made to have the letters fit (for example, Calgary has a *C* in it and Regina has an *R* in it — *YQR*), but the ICAO spokesperson remarks that this couldn't be done in all cases.

Q. What can you tell me about a Canadian passenger aircraft that was bombed in the 1940s?

A. The incident you probably refer to is a Quebec Airlines flight leaving from Montreal on September 9, 1949. The aircraft exploded in mid air. A bomb had been placed in a baggage compartment, and the explosion killed all twenty-three passengers.

The subsequent investigation identified one of the dead as Rita Guay. A couple of weeks later, police arrested her husband, Albert, and charged him with murder. It seems that Guay had two accomplices, his mistress, Marguerite Pitre, and her brother, Genéréux Ruest. Pitre had owed money to Albert Guay, and one of her tasks was getting the dynamite for him and delivering a parcel containing the bomb to the airport. Ruest had a workshop that made the timing device for the bomb.

Guay's motivation was to collect the insurance money upon his wife's death. After he was convicted in 1950, he made a full confession and implicated his two accomplices. Guay was hanged in 1951, while Pitre and Ruest were later found guilty and also hanged.

Q. On the first moon walk Apollo astronauts left messages behind from every country. What did Canada's say?

A: Astronauts Neil Armstrong and Buzz Aldrin left messages on the moon's surface on a grey disc the size of a half dollar. The bilingual message from then Prime Minister Pierre Trudeau was: "Man reached out and touched the tranquil moon. Puisse ce haut fait permettre à l'homme de redécouvrir la terre et d'y trouver la paix." The French translates as "May that high accomplishment allow man to rediscover the earth and there find peace."

Q. Is it fact or fiction that Canadian beer is stronger than American beer?

A. We have all heard it said, and most of us have probably said it ourselves while imbibing south of the border: American beer tastes like water compared to our home-brewed variety.

But while regular Canadian beer contains 0.5 per cent more alcohol than U.S. beer, a spokesperson for the Brewers Association of Canada declares that Canadian beer's more

A glass of beer.

[Brewers Association of Canada]

full-bodied flavour is the result of its ingredients rather than of the extra alcohol.

"Canadian beer has that distinct, different taste mainly because we use 50 per cent more malt barley than the Americans," he says. "It's a vital component in our beer. The Americans use more corn."

The spokesperson adds that regular Canadian beer has an alcohol-by-volume content of 5 per cent (with some stronger exceptions), while U.S. beer registers at 4.5 per cent. Canadian light beer tends to be 4 per cent alcohol while American light beer is 3.8 per cent.

Cheers!

Q. Who are the people responsible for the Gideon Bibles found in hotel rooms across Canada?

A. The Bibles are placed in hotel rooms by Gideons International in Canada, says its national promotion co-ordinator. He doesn't know how many Bibles are placed there each year, but the Gideons have distributed more than 1.1 million Bibles in Canadian hotels since they began the service in 1911.

Members of the chapters or "camps" of Gideons across Canada are responsible for contacting local hotels to ensure that Bibles are placed in each room. About 95 per cent of Canadian hotels have Bibles, and those that refuse them do so, he says, because of the religion of the management or owner. Some hotels, such as the Journey's End chain, contact the Gideons' head office in Guelph, Ontario, each year stating how many hotels they plan to open, their location, and how to contact the manager so that the Bibles can be in the rooms when the hotel opens.

There are about 170,000 members worldwide who distribute Bibles in 148 countries. The version found in most Canadian hotels is the New American Standard Bible.

The Gideons began in the United States in 1899 as a group of travelling salesmen; they were Christians who met regularly for association and friendship.

"They wondered what they could do of a tangible nature as a group to help their fellow citizens," explains the spokesperson. Because salesmen were often on the road for weeks at a time and staying in hotels, they began in 1908 in the United States to place Bibles in those establishments. The first Canadian chapter was formed in 1911 in Toronto.

Much of the money from the Gideons' fund-raising campaign goes toward the Bible program. The money is raised through its Memorial Bible Plan, from member donations and from contributions by other Christian groups.

Of course, Bibles are often taken from the hotels. The people responsible for putting them there in the first place check with the hotels every six months to a year to see if replacements are needed. Bibles that aren't taken are usually replaced after about ten years.

The Gideons' head office gets letters weekly from people thanking them for the service as well as letters from those who have taken Bibles from hotels.

The spokesperson comments: "The letters are usually along the lines of 'I took this Bible a long time ago,' and what they are saying is 'my conscience has bothered me and here is $25 to pay for it.'" The organization doesn't mind if Bibles are removed from the room, because "we assume they are taking it for a reason."

Q. Is the World's Biggest Bookstore in Toronto really what it claims to be?

A. It depends on how you look at it. A merchandise manager for the store told us, "To the best of our knowledge we are the world's biggest bookstore." The store, which celebrates its sixteenth anniversary in November 1996, has 76,000 square feet of selling space, something in the neighbourhood of twelve miles of shelving, and more than one million books within the store.

Nevertheless, the store is not listed in the *Guinness Book of World Records*. The book lists W. and G. Foyle Ltd. of London, England as having the most titles and the longest shelving space (thirty miles). The square footage is listed as 75,825. The book also lists the Barnes and Noble Bookstore in New York City as having the most square footage at 154,250 and 12.87 miles of shelving.

The manager believes, however, that the Barnes and Noble people base their figures on their main store as well as an annex store across the street. Because the World's Biggest Bookstore is all in one building, he stands by his company's claim.

Q. *What is the story behind the cholera epidemic in Canada in the nineteenth century?*

A. The disease, which could kill people within hours when the body became dehydrated through vicious attacks of diarrhea, is estimated to have taken eight thousand lives in Canada between 1831 and 1852.

Ottawa historian Hugh A. Halliday notes that the illness reached epidemic proportions in 1832, 1834, 1849, and 1854. Severe outbreaks in 1851-52 were confined to Quebec.

Halliday says that Asiatic cholera emerged in India in 1826, raged through Europe and the United Kingdom by 1831, and eventually reached Upper and Lower Canada when ships loaded with Irish, Scots, and English immigrants arrived in Canada in 1832.

While some ships were clean and spacious, others were filthy and crammed with people carrying cholera. As the voyages progressed toward North America, the death tolls mounted and bodies were thrown overboard to the sharks.

On April 28, 1832, a ship called the *Constantina* arrived at Grosse Île, Quebec, after losing 29 of its 199 passengers to the disease. Authorities, who had scant knowledge of cholera, set up an ill-managed quarantine station which, not surprisingly, failed to block the spread of the disease from ships to towns.

On June 8, 1832, the disease arrived in Quebec City and within three months more than 2,200 cholera victims were buried. In the same period, about 1,840 people died in Montreal. Victims in cities had the dignity of graves, but in Grosse Île the dead immigrants were buried en masse in pits. In Toronto (then known as York), 192 people died, and in London, Ontario, there were also victims.

As is usually the case when disaster strikes, the government of the day was accused of ineptitude for its handling of the matter. Political radicals alleged that the disease was being used to decimate the French population, but on a personal level Canadians rallied to help the sick and adopt orphans, according to Halliday, showing they were wiser and more compassionate than bureaucrats and demagogues.

Q. If Toronto's CN Tower were to fall over, how far would it reach?

A: Unless you live within its shadow, you probably don't have to cower in fear. However, the world's tallest free-standing structure rises 1,815 feet, 5 inches (553.3 metres), or about one-third of a mile, above downtown Toronto near the corner of Front and John streets.

The tower was built with reinforced steel and concrete to withstand winds of more than two hundred

The CN Tower, Toronto, Ontario.

[Mark Kearney]

miles per hour. If it ever did topple over to the south, however, it would crash through the Gardiner Expressway and reach into Lake Ontario. If it fell north, it would squash the city's Convention Centre and fall about four city blocks to King Street. Toppling east, it would cover about three and a half blocks, almost touching Union Station, while pitching over to the west the tower would slice a path through the Skydome stadium and reach to Spadina Avenue.

It is not likely to happen, but the scenario does make a good plot for a trashy B-movie horror flick.

Q: Is it true that the world's largest cheese was made in Canada?

A: While Canada could once lay claim to that feat, the answer now is no. The world's largest cheese was made in Wisconsin in 1988 and weighed more than forty thousand pounds. It was later exhibited throughout the United States.

Canada, however, was no slouch in this department either. In 1893, a cheese was made in Perth, Ontario, that was six feet tall, twenty-eight feet around, and weighed eleven tons (or twenty-two thousand pounds). It's estimated that it would have taken a person eating a pound a day 423 years to clean the plate. The cheese was taken by rail car to the World's Fair in Chicago and was so heavy it fell through the floor of one of the pavilions.

Q. Whatever happened to the custom-built car called the 67X that was used as a promotion for Canada's Centennial in 1967?

A. There wasn't just one, there were four custom-built cars known as the 67X. The cars were commissioned by Esso in 1967 as part of their sales promotions for Canada's centennial. The 67Xs were unveiled in the spring of that year; their code name in the company was "Bubbles."

The 67X was designed by a Californian, George Barris, who had also built the original Batmobile, the hot-rod hearse used by TV's The Munsters, and special cars for such Hollywood stars as Frank Sinatra and Dean Martin.

The 67X was based on a GM design and was built lower than a Volkswagen and longer than a Cadillac. Two of the cars were gold coloured, one was avocado green and the other a burgundy red.

Some of the 67X's features were air-foam-padded seats, a swiveling passenger seat, stereo tape decks in the front and rear, individual reading lights, an inside and outside thermometer, and a recessed dash instrument panel of Brazilian walnut. The cars came complete with the GM warranty.

They were given out as prizes by Esso during the Centennial year, with the winners being from what was then Fort William (now Thunder Bay), Ontario, Okanagan Landing, British Columbia, St. Romauld, Quebec, and Edmonton, Alberta. Only the Edmonton winner kept his car; the other three put theirs up for sale immediately. Although it is difficult to determine the 67X's value today, one of the sellers was asking $25,000 back in 1967.

As to what has happened to the cars, one of them — the burgundy red 67X — was purchased in 1976 by Robert Domik of Niagara Falls. In a newspaper article from a few years ago, Domik mentioned that he spent time restoring his car and has displayed it at some auto shows in the Niagara region and in the United States.

He was quoted in the article as saying he believed only three of the cars have survived. Besides his, one was in western Canada and the other in the States.

Q. What was the best year to be born in Canada?

A. As far as demographers can tell to date, the best year to have been born in Canada in the twentieth century, especially with regard to supply and demand in the workplace, was 1938.

John Kettle, author of the book *The Big Generation* and a consulting futurist, asserts that 1938 was a good year because so few people, relatively speaking, were born in Canada in that year. Because much of what happens to you is based on age (for example, age often determines when you enter the work force, when you are at your peak buying power, when you reach the highest position at a job, etc.), he explains that demographers have looked at birth rates for various years and then examined the population twenty years later.

The twenty-year-age figures are used because it is roughly at that age people enter the labour force.

In 1958, people who were twenty years old made up about 1.5 per cent of the population, writes Kettle, and that was the lowest percentage for any birth year examined. "There were fewer people in relation to the population then, and so you were in demand."

He contrasts these figures with those for people born in the early 1950s, during the baby boom. Twenty years later in the 1970s, this group made up about 2 per cent of the population. Although the difference doesn't seem great, it means that about one-third more people of that age were looking for a job in those years than their counterparts in 1958.

Another great year to be born was 1970, according to Kettle, because as of 1990, people who were twenty made up only 1.3 per cent of the total population — even less than the figures for those born in 1938. It is still too early in this age group's lives, though, to determine what the future holds economically. They are entering the work force at a time when the Canadian economy is weak. Kettle thinks they may have to weather a few tough years, but could then find themselves in demand in the work force for much of their lives, because of their relatively small numbers.

Q. Have Canadians always driven cars on the right-hand side of the road?

A. That's a simple enough question, but the answer is difficult to pin down. Officials at the Canadian Automotive Museum in Oshawa, Ontario, state that most cars built before 1914 were right-hand drive (that is, primarily designed for driving on the left side of the road). Eventually, car manufacturers started changing over to left-hand drive (what we have today), perhaps because Henry Ford had started building his cars that way and they were proving popular. Canadians may have been used to driving on the left side of the road because of their strong ties to Great Britain, where people still drive on the left. In fact, according to *A Short History of Early Cars, Racing and Touring in Canada*, the Maritimes didn't abandon driving on the left side of the road until 1923.

Jack Crawford, an automobile historian from Sarnia, Ontario, provided information showing that the concept of left-hand drive (i.e. cars that are better suited to being driven on the right side of the road) came into vogue in the United States about 1908. Nevertheless, cars with the steering wheel on the right-hand side continued to be produced as well.

As has often been the case, Canadians followed a trend prevailing in America: driving on the same side of the road was less confusing, especially for people living near the border.

As for the reason why North America had followed the British idea of right-hand drive in the first place, Crawford provided an article that mentions that British cars were looked upon as superior in the early days of the twentieth century. The article also explains how driving on the left side of the road got started in Britain. It seems that the "Keep Left" rule was traditional in Great Britain and was made law in 1835. Although most of Europe had wide open roads, Britain's roads were relatively narrow and heavily treed on either side. Horsemen wanted to keep the right or sword arm free in case of battle and this meant keeping to the left. And when the horse-drawn carriage took over, drivers wanted to keep their whip hand free.

Today, most of the world, including Canada, drives on the right, but such places as Great Britain, Australia, and Japan are exceptions.

Q. How heavy are the furry caps worn by guards at the Change of the Guard ceremony on Parliament Hill in Ottawa?

A. They may look like they weigh a ton, but the caps worn by the Ceremonial Guard are about 18 inches high, 12 inches wide and tip the scales at only 12 to 14 ounces.

They are made from Canadian black bearskin stretched over a wicker or bamboo framework and attached to a leather harness, which fits over the top of the head and is held in place by a chain worn between the lower lip and chin.

Changing the Guard, Ottawa, Canada.
[Ottawa Tourism & Convention Authority]

A lieutenant at CFB Ottawa South explained that the key to wearing the lofty caps is balancing them properly on the head. The headgear is worn by about 150 guards and band members who perform in the daily ceremony on the Parliament Hill lawn between June and August.

The colourful ceremony, which is viewed by about five thousand people a day, changes the guard at the Ottawa residence of the governor general. It is derived from the changing-the-guard ceremony at Buckingham Palace in London, England.

Use of the caps dates back to 1815, at the Battle of Waterloo, when British troops defeated Napoleon's Imperial Guard, whose members were wearing bearskin caps. Because they won the historic fight, the British were allowed to wear the bearskins, and the tradition has continued until today.

Q. Does the difference between the Imperial gallon and the American gallon have its origin in the American Revolution?

A. Indirectly, yes. But while you might think that the Americans did the changing, the opposite is true. Prior to the Revolution, Americans had adopted most of the measurements of Old England. At that time there were two gallons used by the English — the ale gallon and the wine gallon (which was slightly smaller) — and the Americans adopted the latter.

Apparently, the English decided in 1824 to punish the Americans for the Revolution by switching from the two-tier system of gallons. They decided to create the British Imperial gallon which was the equivalent of 10 pounds of water at a temperature of 62 degrees Fahrenheit.

Americans did not go along with the switch, but retained their Old English measurements. Of course, as more countries, including Canada and perhaps someday the United States, switch to metric, the whole tradition of difference may become a thing of the past.

Q. How many people touch a piece of mail sent from, say, Toronto to Vancouver?

A. Since the post office mechanized its sorting process in the late sixties and early seventies, human hands have had considerably less contact with the mail. A Canada Post spokesperson in Ottawa tells us that, with today's technology, as few as four people will actually touch a letter from the moment it is dropped into a mail box in Toronto, until it is placed in a mail box in Vancouver.

The first point of human contact is the postal employee who clears the mailbox where the letter was deposited. The piece of mail is then transported to a mail sorting plant, where machinery takes over for the next few steps. It is mechanically deposited into a machine which cancels the stamp, before being automatically sorted on another machine.

The human touch re-enters the picture when a postal worker takes the letter off the sorting machine in bundle form and places it into a wire cage for transport to Vancouver. The cage is loaded onto a truck and eventually moved to an airplane for its flight west.

In Vancouver, it is sorted by machine into a letter carrier's "walk" and then human hands place it into a bin to await the carrier. The final set of hands to make contact — other than yours when you rip open the letter — are those of the carrier who places the letter in your mail box.

The spokesperson adds that mechanization of the post office did not reduce jobs at the post office. The introduction of postal codes, however, did result in a leaner work force at Canada Post, and the introduction of more electronic equipment is expected to cut other jobs.

Q. Is the miniskirt a Canadian invention?

A. Fashion experts may be surprised to hear it but yes, there is evidence that the short skirts that have turned many a man's head were invented in Canada.

Historian W. J. Eccles made the point in a letter to the editor in the *Globe and Mail* on June 8, 1977. Wrote Eccles: "The truth of the matter is that the mini-skirt was a Canadian invention; it came into vogue with the womanfolk of New France (later Quebec) in the first half of the eighteenth century.

"The observant Peter Kalm, professor of botany at Uppsala University, during his 1749 visit to Canada in the interests of science commented in his journal on this intriguing mode of dress. On July 25, he wrote: 'Every day but Sunday they [Canadian women] wear a little neat jacket and a short skirt which hardly reaches halfway down the leg and sometimes not that far.'"

Q. How many museums are there in Canada?

A. According to the *Official Directory of Canadian Museums*, there are more than two thousand museums across the country. Some of them are huge, such as the Canadian Museum of Civilization in Hull, Quebec, while some take up a few square feet in the corner of a building.

And Canada certainly has its share of the weird and wonderful when it comes to museums. One of these listed in the directory is the Donalda and District Museum in Donalda, Alberta, which houses 700 lamps and 360 pairs of salt and pepper shakers. The Ontario Puppetry Association

Canadian Museum of Civilization, Hull.
[Ottawa Tourism & Convention Authority]

Puppet Centre in Willowdale, Ontario, features more than 500 puppets from around the world.

And another one you might want to keep on your list of places to visit is the International Fox Hall of Fame and Museum in Summerside, Prince Edward Island, which depicts the fox industry that was established near there a century ago.

Who knows what kind of souvenirs you might pick up at these places ...

Q. How did my favourite drink, Newfoundland Screech, get its name?

A. We hope you'll toast our answer.

Jamaican rum has long been a mainstay in Newfoundland, having been acquired originally in exchange for salt fish. According to the Newfoundland Liquor Corporation, the government took over control of the liquor business in the early twentieth century and began selling rum in unlabelled bottles.

During World War II, an American serviceman was having his first taste of the rum and downed his drink in one gulp. Apparently, he let out such a loud howl that many locals came running to see what was the matter. An American sergeant arrived on the scene and demanded to know what "that ungodly screech" was. The serviceman's Newfoundlander host replied "The screech? 'Tis the rum, me son."

The legend surrounding the drink's origin was born. The liquor board pounced on the new name and began labelling the rum Screech.

Q. What is the Order of Canada and who receives it?

A. The Order of Canada was established on July 1, 1967, Canada's one-hundreth birthday, to honour Canadians who have made outstanding contributions at the international, national or local level. The Order of Canada, according to government literature, "is a fraternity of merit, not a society of the elite" and brings no special privileges and no monetary reward.

The honour is split into three categories — Companion, Officer and Member — in order to embrace a spectrum of achievement and service. The Companion level recognizes international service or achievement, or national pre-eminence; the Officer level recognizes national service or achievement; and the Member level recognizes outstanding contributions at the local or regional level.

Anyone may propose the name of a deserving Canadian as a candidate for appointment by contacting Rideau Hall, the Ottawa residence of the governor general, who gives out the honours twice annually, on New Year's Day and Canada Day. The Constitution of the Order allows the appointment of 150 Companions, 46 Officers and 92 Members each year.

The list of recipients of the Order of Canada over the past several years reads like a Canadian who's who. Those to receive the Order include: actors Christopher Plummer and Donald Sutherland; artists Harold Town and Alexander

Colville; the late broadcaster Barbara Frum; Toronto entrepreneur "Honest" Ed Mirvish; pianist Oscar Peterson; country singer Stompin' Tom Connors; three members of the Toronto rock band Rush; historian Desmond Morton; Ernest Coombs, better known as children's entertainer Mr. Dressup; Olympians Alex Baumann, Nancy Greene and Brian Orser; hockey players Wayne Gretzky, Gordie Howe, Phil Esposito and Bobby Orr; recording artists Bryan Adams, David Foster and Anne Murray, and writers Margaret Atwood, Pierre Berton, Robertson Davies and Peter C. Newman.

Q. Who decides what subjects are commemorated on postage stamps?

A. Believe it or not — you too could have your idea appear on a Canadian stamp. Subject matter for stamp designs comes from books, encyclopedias, newspapers, magazines, and yes, the general public, says a Canada Post spokesperson.

To start with, Canada Post staff comb through as much printed matter as possible searching for anniversaries and upcoming Canadian events worthy of celebration on a stamp. The post office also invites suggestions from various experts, organizations, and the public, she explained, and receives between eighty to a hundred unsolicited ideas every month.

Several thousand suggestions are narrowed down to about one hundred, which are considered by an eleven-member committee with expertise in philately, history, law, art, and other disciplines.

The committee bases its decisions on a corporate policy which aims for stamp subjects of national significance in categories like history, accomplishments, natural heritage, social development, culture, economic life, and may include people who have made outstanding contributions in their field.

In order to put the significance of a person's contribution into a historical perspective, individuals aren't honoured on a stamp until at least ten years after their death. No living person except the reigning monarch may be so commemorated.

The stamp committee meets twice a year to review and discuss all proposed subjects before making recommendations to the board of directors for final approval.

Up to forty individual stamp designs are printed annually.

If your suggestion is accepted, don't expect to see it on a stamp a month later. It can take up to three years before your design is issued and stuck on letters and parcels.

Postage stamps have been in use in Canada since 1851. Today, all Canadian stamps are printed in Toronto and Ottawa.

Confederation stamps issued by the Post Office Department, Ottawa, Ontario, July 1927.

Q. How does Canada's postal code work?

A. The first of a postal code's six characters identifies the province, or part of a province, that is the letter's destination. The second stands for a community or section of a community within the province, and the third describes a certain area in the city or community.

In Saskatoon's case, for example, the letter *S* which begins each postal code in the city, signifies the province of Saskatchewan. The number, in the first trio of characters (a seven), identifies Saskatoon as the city the mail is headed for, and the final letter, such as an *H*, *J*, *K*, *M*, *N*, or *L*, specifies a certain neighbourhood.

The second set of characters — a number, a letter and a number — is even more specific. It can identify the side of a street between intersections, a building occupied by a business, an apartment, a large volume mailer within a building, or a cluster of lock boxes in the lobby of a building.

The letters *D*, *F*, *I*, *O*, *Q* and *U* are not used in any postal codes because they resemble other letters or numbers, according to Canada Post. *E* and *F*, for example, are similar, as are *I* and *1*. Letters *W* and *Z* are being held in reserve in anticipation of a need for more postal codes at some time in the future.

And you thought they were adding those letters and numbers just to give you more work to do ...

Q. If a pregnant woman gives birth in an airplane after it leaves the ground, what is the child's registered birthplace?

A. If the plane has taken off from Alberta, for example, and a baby is born in the air, its birth certificate will say it was born at the first community where the airplane landed, according to a spokesperson for the vital statistics branch of the Alberta Department of Health.

In other words, if a baby is born ten minutes after its mother's Winnipeg-bound flight leaves Calgary Airport, the child's birth certificate will say Winnipeg was the birthplace, if the plane touches down at Winnipeg. If the flight happens to make a stop in Regina first, that will be the infant's place of birth.

The same holds true for a Saskatchewan-based departure, but a spokesperson there notes there could be exceptions. If someone knew exactly where the plane was located when the child was born — over Swift Current, for example — the baby could be registered as being born there.

"If there is uncertainty, it is sensible to register the child where the plane lands," he said. "But we would look at each individual case."

Ontario has a similar approach, but the custom does not apply to babies born on ships. Their birthplace is recorded as the port where the ship is registered. If a baby is born on an Amsterdam, Netherlands-registered ship as it chugs its way across Lake Ontario, the child's birthplace is Amsterdam. So it appears in Section 28 of the Ontario Vital Statistics Act.

Q. Is Quebec the only province where it is against the law to turn right on all red lights?

A. You can make a right turn on most red lights in every province or territory in Canada with the exception of Quebec, where it is illegal to turn on all reds. If you are caught doing it in La Belle Province, you'll get a ticket, probably for around $150, depending on highway traffic regulations in the municipality where the infraction occurs.

A Quebec Transport Ministry spokesperson said that right turns on red lights have always been banned as a method of preventing pedestrian-car accidents. A transit commission in the Ottawa-Hull area has asked Quebec to change the law to help buses move through traffic, but the spokesperson believed it was not likely to happen.

Another ministry official commented that American studies show an increase in pedestrian-car mishaps following the abolition of the right-turn ban.

Q. What can you tell me about Canada's railway post offices?

A. A railway post office was a post office on wheels which was pulled around Canada until the early seventies as part of the freight and passenger trains that crisscrossed the country every day.

The rolling postal stations took up full rail cars (sixty feet in length), half cars (thirty feet) or quarter cars (fifteen feet) and included space for storing and sorting mail, plus toilets and cooking facilities. The post office leased the cars from the railroad on which they operated on a per mile basis.

For more than a century, wherever there was track, the mail went by train. As soon as a rail line opened, a postal car was added to the train travelling that line.

The railway post office system was the subject of considerable praise in its day as it allowed for continuity in the flow of mail because letters and parcels were loaded onto trains and sorted en route to their destination and also because personnel were highly trained and efficient.

Documentation provided by the National Postal Museum in Ottawa points out, "The mail was never delayed in a terminal for a day or longer. For instance, it arrived in Winnipeg from the four points of the compass, sorted and ready to be loaded onto several waiting trains for onward transmission, and never saw the Winnipeg post office. It was delivered to the addressee in Vancouver three days later, in Halifax four days later.

"Try to match that today, even with the assistance of postal codes and state-of-the-art technology," writes former railway mail clerk André Joseph Janssens, who travelled more than one million miles in western Canada, northwestern Ontario, and parts of Minnesota between 1943 and 1971.

Railway mail died in 1971 when trucks and airplanes replaced trains as carriers of the mail.

Q. Remembrance Day ceremonies commemorate the First World War ending on the eleventh hour of the eleventh day of the eleventh month. But in what time zone was that eleventh hour?

A. Although people across Canada celebrate Remembrance Day on November 11 and pay tribute with a minute's silence at 11:00 A.M., the time the war ended officially wouldn't have been at 11:00 A.M. in this country.

According to a spokesperson for the Royal Canadian Legion in Ottawa, the decision to end the war at 11:00 A.M. was based on Greenwich Mean Time. That means the war officially ended in Europe at that time, but because Canada has different time zones and lies a number of hours away from Greenwich time, the actual hour the war ended would differ.

For example, it would have been 6:00 A.M. in Ontario when the Armistice was reached. In British Columbia it would have been 3:00 A.M. because Pacific time is eight hours behind Greenwich. The spokesperson added, however, that it was agreed that each section of the country would have its minute of silence at 11:00 A.M. local time.

Q. Why is someone from Calgary called a Calgarian? Is there a formula that determines how to refer to a resident of a particular town or city?

A. In his book *Speaking Canadian English* (1970), lawyer and linguist Mark M. Orkin gives some general rules governing the designation of a community's residents.

Orkin's formula is as follows:

If the name ends in *a*, add an *n*. That makes an Ottawa resident an Ottawan. If the name of your city ends in *ia*, also add an *n*. An Orillia resident is an Orillian. If the name ends in a *y*, like Calgary, for instance, change the *y* to an *i*, add *an* and become a Calgarian.

If a community's name ends in *on*, add *ian*. Edmonton folks, are Edmontonians. If the name ends in *outh*, such as Dartmouth, add *ian*, for Dartmouthian. If a name ends with a vowel other than *a*, add *ite*, sometimes with a hyphen, sometimes without; so we have Barrie-ites and Nanaimoites. And if a name ends with a consonant, in some cases, add *er*, to make Londoner. In other cases add *ite*, such as in Windsorite or Markhamite.

There are, of course, exceptions. People in Oakville, for example, probably refer to themselves as Oakvillians, says a spokesperson for the town. Toronto ends in a vowel other than an *a*, but Toronto residents are known as Torontonians, not Torontoites. And the residents of Woodstock, Ontario, who should be called Woodstockers or Woodstockites according to Orkin's formula, are in reality known as Woodstonians. And people from Halifax are called Haligonians.

Q. Is the snowblower an invention we can attribute to someone from the Great White North?

A. The snowblower, that great preventer of backaches, is, in fact, a Canadian invention. Its creator was Arthur Sicard, a Montreal-area farm boy-turned entrepreneur, who tired of having his milk spoil whenever the roads to market were blocked by snow drifts, which happened frequently.

In the late 1800s he experimented with a variety of snow-removal techniques — including scrapers and V-shaped plows attached to automobiles — all to no avail. His idea for a snowblower was sparked by a farm threshing machine, which consisted of revolving metal "worms" and a fan which blew chopped-up straw up a pipe into a strawstack.

Sicard invested his meager savings in a truck with primitive worms and a blower. It worked on small drifts but broke down on larger ones. When Sicard left farming for the construction business, the idea went on hold until twenty years later when he owned his own company and had enough cash to return to his idea.

With stronger gasoline engines on the market, he sank $40,000 into his first hand-built blower, and it rumbled onto the streets of Montreal in 1924. He patented his invention in the late 1920s and sold his first machine for $13,000 through his own incorporated company. He sold machines to the Quebec department of highways, the city of

Montreal and the St. Hubert airport, and eventually his work force increased to 160 as production jumped to fifty-six units a year.

Sicard died of a heart attack in 1946, just as his Sicard snowblowers were becoming familiar sights across North America.

Q. Do the digits in my Social Insurance Number (SIN) mean anything?

A. If you are wondering whether the government, or anyone else for that matter, can look at your SIN and tell which political party you voted for or how much money you earn, rest easy. The numbers don't mean anything specific, says a government spokesperson, although the first three digits do identify the province you lived in when your number was issued.

He adds that a SIN can also be used to track a person down, but only if proper channels are used. The RCMP alone is allowed to use a SIN for such purposes.

If the first three numbers of your card are in the 100s, it was issued in the Maritimes; the 200s, Quebec; the 400s and 500s, Ontario; 600s, Saskatchewan, Manitoba and Alberta; 700s British Columbia, Yukon, and Northwest Territories. Numbers in the 300s have been reserved for Quebec, which is almost out of 200s, and numbers beginning in the 900s are for people who are not Canadian citizens but who require a SIN to go to university or deal with a bank.

The official explained that SINs are closely guarded and can only be linked with a name by the RCMP, according to agreements between the federal solicitor general's office and various government departments. If, for example, you have marked personal property with your SIN, and it is stolen and recovered, a local police force cannot identify you as the owner without contacting the RCMP.

The numbers were introduced in 1964 as identifiers for people registering for the Canada Pension Plan and unemployment insurance. Before that, three digits and a letter had been used as the UIC identifier. In 1967, Revenue Canada began using SINs to keep track of people filing income tax returns, and in the years since then a variety of other government bodies and acts, including the Canada Elections Act, have also gained the authority to ask Canadians for their SIN.

Q. Where is Canada's only free-standing stone spiral staircase located?

A. The staircase you speak of is located in the Saint John County Court building in New Brunswick and was built in the early 1800s. It loops from the ground floor of the building to the judges' chamber at the top and is made up of granite stairs constructed from stone from Scotland, a wooden banister, and a wrought-iron railing.

The courthouse that houses the staircase is a National Historic Site built for the shiretown of Saint John and included a city courtroom, a circuit court, and a common council chamber. In 1919 the Great Fire swept through the building destroying everything but the walls and the spiral staircase. The staircase was restored to its original state a few years ago.

Q. Are there more Canadian tea drinkers than coffee drinkers?

A. According to the Tea and Coffee Association of Canada, coffee drinkers outnumber their tea counterparts by about five to one. Approximately 55 to 60 per cent of Canadians drink coffee, and the average Canadian coffee drinker downs about three and three-quarter cups per day.

But the executive director of the Tea Council of Canada says statistics can be misleading. Although the amount of coffee consumed outside the house may be five times greater than that of tea, the latter more than holds its own with coffee when you look at drinks consumed at home. The amount of tea sipped per capita is about ten a week, he informs us, but that includes the entire population, not exclusively tea drinkers.

In addition, tea is enjoying something of a resurgence, he adds. Tea is becoming more visible in retail shops and restaurants, and many places are now offering afternoon tea as a daily ritual.

Tea was the most popular beverage in Canada in the 1950s and 1960s, he points out, and he expects consumption to grow in the 1990s as baby boomers get older. As people become increasingly health-conscious, yearning for a slower pace of life and looking for entertainment at home rather than away from it, tea consumption could go up.

"Tea fits [the lifestyle]," says the director. "You take a break with tea. It's relaxing, it's something you do for yourself. You don't have tea on the run."

Coffee mug and tea cup.

Q. Do the numbers of my telephone area code actually mean anything?

A: Area codes came into existence in 1947, and there are currently more than 150 different ones throughout Canada and the United States. All area codes generally have a 0 or a 1 as their middle number. At the same time, the first three digits of your phone number after the area code, until recently, never had a 0 or a 1 in the middle.

That system was set up to allow the electronic gadgetry to recognize that the number you are dialing is long distance. A researcher for Bell Canada in Montreal explains that when the first area codes were assigned in 1947, numbers that had a 0 in the middle were reserved for those states or provinces that had only one area code.

The states or provinces that had a large enough population to warrant more than one area code within their borders were assigned area codes with a 1 in the middle. Hence, Mississauga, which is in a highly populated part of Ontario, had an area code with a 1 in it, 416.

Because of the growing number of telephones in use (in cars, briefcases, and so forth), a change was made, however, and Mississauga as well as other parts of Ontario near Toronto were assigned a new area code, 905, in 1993.

"As for the first and third numbers of the code, from what I can tell from the research, it seems that they were assigned arbitrarily," remarks the researcher.

Those numbers do, however, tell the gadgetry what geographical region of North America you are calling.

Something to ponder the next time you are put on hold.

Q. What was Canada's connection to the world system of time zones?

A. A Canadian, Sir Sandford Fleming, was instrumental in the development of the system of time zones used around the world. In the nineteenth century, the advent of rapid railway and telegraph communications made obsolete the

Sandford Fleming, C.M.G.

[NAC/PA-C14238]

system whereby every major centre set its clocks according to local astronomical conditions.

An American, Charles Ferdinand Dowd, encouraged U.S. railways to recognize uniform time zones, but Fleming took the concept a step further by advocating use of the principle on an international scale. Fleming was largely responsible for convening an international conference in Washington in 1884 at which the system of international standard time with twenty-four time zones was adopted. The system is still in use today.

Q. Who first had the idea of painting dotted white lines down the centre of highways?

A. There are apparently a number of claimants to the title throughout North America, but some experts say those dotted lines got their start near the Quebec-Ontario border. An information officer with Ontario's Ministry of

White lines on a road.

[Photo: Catherine Blake]

Transportation agrees with the theory that a young Ontario engineer, J.D. Millar, painted the white lines back in 1930 to help guide drivers when fog drifted in.

"Between 1919 and 1930 a lot of bright lights (in Canada and the United States) came up with the idea of putting white lines on the road," he says, "but I believe Millar was the first one to actually do it." There was a rapid increase in the number of vehicles on the road during the twenties which also increased the need for safe paved roads.

According to the book *A New Day For Roads*, Millar's boss thought the idea was dumb and ordered the white lines removed. But within three years, the dotted lines had become standard in North America. Millar later became deputy minister of the Department of Highways.

Q. What can you tell me about the origin of Canadian whisky?

A. The first Canadian whiskies were made in the 1700s by newly arrived settlers from the British Isles and Loyalists from the south, according to information provided by the Liquor Control Board of Ontario. Many turned to farming for their livelihood and grew corn and rye. In the fall, with the harvest gathered, they erected stills and turned excess grain into whisky, as solace for the long winter ahead and as an item to trade.

As settlements grew, millers and merchants drew on their entrepreneurial spirit to build distilleries beside their mills and began producing larger quantities of whisky. By the 1860s, William Gooderham and James Worts had established distilleries in Toronto, as had Henry Corby in Belleville and Hiram Walker across the river from Detroit, near what is now Windsor. The Waterloo Distillery, eventual keystone of the Seagram's empire, was also set up.

In 1874, Canadian whisky was officially recognized as distinct from its southern competitors, although it is hard to pinpoint why, until Hiram Walker developed a new blend of rye whisky and neutral spirits much lighter and cleaner than American straight rye, with a full flavour. He sold it in labelled bottles rather than anonymous kegs and named it Canadian Club. Canadian Club was a big hit in Europe and the United States, and other distilleries soon adopted Walker's ideas, developing their own distinctly Canadian brands.

Q. Why do Canadians pronounce the last letter of the alphabet as "zed" while Americans say "zee"?

A. The letter is derived from the Greek "zeta," which was later adopted by the French who pronounced it as zed. This pronunciation was also used in Britain where it remains the standard way of saying the letter.

In parts of Britain, however, such as Suffolk and Norfolk, the letter was further abbreviated in pronunciation to zee. It was from those regions of Britain that many people emigrated to the United States. In contrast, many settlers coming to Canada were Scots or Irish, or originated from English regions where the zed pronunciation was common.

In 1828, Noah Webster produced his famous American Dictionary of the English Language. Webster was very much in favour of making the American form of English distinct from British usage. He wrote "Our honor requires us to have a system of our own, in language as well as government. Thus, he adopted the pronunciation "zee" which was common in the United States by then.

Webster also dropped the *u* from many words such as colour and honour, turned "tyre" into "tire" and "theatre" into "theater." Canadians remained loyal to the British spelling and pronunciations. Although we have since adopted or come to accept some of the American spellings, we still hang on to zed.